JOSHUA AND
THE JUDGES

The Bible for School and Home

by J. Paterson Smyth

The Book of Genesis

Moses and the Exodus

Joshua and the Judges

The Prophets and Kings

When the Christ Came:
The Highlands of Galilee

When the Christ Came:
The Road to Jerusalem

St. Matthew

St. Mark

The Bible for School and Home

JOSHUA AND
THE JUDGES

by

J. Paterson Smyth

YESTERDAY'S CLASSICS

ITHACA, NEW YORK

This edition, first published in 2017 by Yesterday's Classics, an imprint of Yesterday's Classics, LLC, is an unabridged republication of the text originally published by Sampson Low, Marston & Co., Ltd. For the complete listing of the books that are published by Yesterday's Classics, please visit www.yesterdaysclassics.com. Yesterday's Classics is the publishing arm of the Baldwin Online Children's Literature Project which presents the complete text of hundreds of classic books for children at www.mainlesson.com.

ISBN: 978-1-63334-019-0

Yesterday's Classics, LLC
PO Box 339
Ithaca, NY 14851

CONTENTS

PART II: THE STORY OF THE JUDGES

GENERAL INTRODUCTION

I

This series of books is intended for two classes of teachers:

1. *For Teachers in Week Day and Sunday Schools.* For these each book is divided into complete lessons. The lesson will demand preparation. Where feasible there should be diligent use of commentaries and of any books indicated in the notes. *As a general rule* I think the teacher should not bring the book at all to his class if he is capable of doing without it. He should make copious notes of the subject. The lesson should be thoroughly studied and digested beforehand, with all the additional aids at his disposal, and it should come forth at the class warm and fresh from his own heart and brain. But I would lay down no rigid rule about the use of the Lesson Book. To some it may be a burden to keep the details of a long lesson in the memory; and, provided the subject has been very carefully studied, the Lesson Book, with its salient points carefully marked in coloured pencil, may be a considerable help. Let each do what seems best in his particular case, only taking care to satisfy his conscience that it is not done through

laziness, and that he can really do best for his class by the plan which he adopts.

2. *For Parents* who would use it in teaching their children at home. They need only small portions, brief little lessons of about ten minutes each night. For these each chapter is divided into short sections. I should advise that on the first night only the Scripture indicated should be read, with some passing remarks and questions to give a grip of the story. That is enough. Then night after night go on with the teaching, taking as much or as little as one sees fit.

I have not written out the teaching in full as a series of readings which could be read over to the child without effort or thought. With this book in hand a very little preparation and adaptation will enable one to make the lesson more interesting and more personal and to hold the child's attention by questioning. Try to get his interest. Try to make him talk. Make the lesson conversational. Don't preach.

II

HINTS FOR TEACHING

An ancient Roman orator once laid down for his pupils the three-fold aim of a teacher:

1. *Placere* (to interest).

2. *Docere* (to teach).

3. *Movere* (to move).

1. To interest the audience (in order to teach them).

2. To teach them (in order to move them).

3. To move them to action.

On these three words of his I hang a few suggestions on the teaching of this set of Lessons.

1. Placere (to interest)

I want especially to insist on attention to this rule. Some teachers seem to think that to interest the pupils is a minor matter. It is not a minor matter and the pupils will very soon let you know it. Believe me, it is no waste of time to spend hours during the week in planning to excite their interest to the utmost. Most of the complaints of inattention would cease at once if the teacher would give more study to rousing their interest. After all, there is little use in knowing the facts of your subject, and being anxious about the souls of the pupils, if all the time that you are teaching, these pupils are yawning and taking no interest in what you say. I know some have more aptitude for teaching than others. Yet, after considerable experience of teachers whose lesson was a weariness to the flesh, and of teachers who never lost attention for a moment, I am convinced, on the whole, that the power to interest largely depends on the previous preparation.

Therefore do not content yourself with merely studying the teaching of this series. Read widely and freely. Read not only commentaries, but books that will give local interest and colour—books that will throw valuable sidelights on your sketch.

But more than reading is necessary. You know the meaning of the expression, *"Put yourself in his place."* Practise that in every Bible story, using your imagination, living in the scene, experiencing, as far as you can, every feeling of the actors. To some this is no effort at all. They feel their cheeks flushing and their eyes growing moist as they project themselves involuntarily into the scene before them. But though it be easier to some than to others, it is in some degree possible to all, and the interest of the lesson largely depends on it. I have done my best in these books to help the teacher in this respect. But no man can help another much. Success will depend entirely on the effort to "put yourself in his place."

In reading the Bible chapter corresponding to each lesson, I suggest that the teacher should read part of the chapter, rather than let the pupils tire themselves by "reading round." My experience is that this "reading round" is a fruitful source of listlessness. When his verse is read, the pupil can let his mind wander till his turn comes again, and so he loses all interest. I have tried, with success, varying the monotony. I would let them read the first round of verses in order; then I would make them read out of the regular order, as I called their names; and sometimes, if the lesson were long, I would again and again interrupt by reading a group of verses myself, making remarks as I went on. To lose their interest is fatal.

I have indicated also in the lessons that you should not unnecessarily give information yourself. Try to question it *into* them. If you tell them facts which they have just read, they grow weary. If you ask a question, and then answer it yourself when they miss it, you cannot keep their attention. Send your questions around in every sort of order, or want of order. Try to puzzle them—try to surprise them. Vary the form of the question, if not answered, and always feel it to be a defeat if you ultimately fail in getting the answer you want.

2. Docere (to teach)

You interest the pupil in order that you may *teach*. Therefore teach definitely the Lesson that is set you. Do not be content with interesting him. Do not be content either with drawing spiritual teaching. Teach the facts before you. Be sure that God has inspired the narration of them for some good purpose.

When you are dealing with Old Testament characters, do not try to shirk or to condone evil in them. They were not faultless saints. They were men like ourselves, whom God was helping and bearing with, as He helps and bears with us, and the interest of the story largely depends on the pupil realizing this.

In the Old Testament books of this series you will find very full chapters written on the Creation, the Fall, the Flood, the election of Jacob, the Sun standing still, the slaughter of Canaanites, and other such subjects. In connection with these I want to say something that especially concerns teachers. Your pupils, now or later, can hardly avoid coming in contact with the flippant scepticism so common nowadays, which makes jests at the story of the sun standing still, and talks of the folly of believing that all humanity was condemned because Eve ate an apple thousands of years ago. This flippant tone is "in the air." They will meet with it in their companions, in the novels of the day, in popular magazine articles on their tables at home. You have, many of you, met with it yourselves; you know how disturbing it is; and you probably know, too, that much of its influence on people arises from the narrow and unwise teaching of the Bible in their youth. Now you have no right to ignore this in your teaching of the Bible. You need not talk of Bible difficulties and their answers. You need not refer to them at all. But teach the truth that will take the sting out of these difficulties when presented in after-life.

To do this requires trouble and thought. We have learned much in the last fifty years that has thrown new light for us on the meaning of some parts of the Bible; which has, at any rate, made doubtful some of our old interpretations of it. We must not ignore this. There are certain traditional theories which some of us still insist on teaching as God's infallible truth, whereas they are really only human opinions about it, which may possibly be mistaken. As long as they are taught as human opinions, even if we are wrong, the mistake will do no harm. But if things are taught as God's infallible truth, to be believed on peril of doubting God's Word, it may do grave mischief, if in after-life the pupil find

6

them seriously disputed, or perhaps false. A shallow, unthinking man, finding part of his teaching false, which has been associated in his mind with the most solemn sanctions of religion, is in danger of letting the whole go. Thus many of our young people drift into hazy doubt about the Bible. Then we get troubled about their beliefs, and give them books of Christian evidences to win them back by explaining that what was taught them in childhood was not *quite* correct, and needs now to be modified by a broader and slightly different view. But we go on as before with the younger generation, and expose them in their turn to the same difficulties.

Does it not strike you that, instead of this continual planning to win men back from unbelief, it might be worth while to try the other method of not exposing them to unbelief? Give them the more careful and intelligent teaching at first, and so prepare them to meet the difficulties by-and-by.

I have no wish to advocate any so-called "advanced" teaching. Much of such teaching I gravely object to. But there are truths of which there is no question amongst thoughtful people, which somehow are very seldom taught to the young, though ignorance about them in after-life leads to grave doubt and misunderstanding. Take, for example, the gradual, progressive nature of God's teaching in Scripture, which makes the Old Testament teaching as a whole lower than that of the New. This is certainly no doubtful question, and the knowledge of it is necessary for an intelligent study of

Scripture. I have dealt with it where necessary in some of the books of this series.

I think, too, our teaching on what may seem to us doubtful questions should be more fearless and candid. If there are two different views each held by able and devout men, do not teach your own as the infallibly true one, and ignore or condemn the other. For example, do not insist that the order of creation must be accurately given in the first chapter of Genesis. You may think so; but many great scholars, with as deep a reverence for the Bible as you have, think that inspired writers were circumscribed by the science of their time. Do not be too positive that the story of the Fall *must be* an exactly literal narrative of facts. If you believe that it is I suppose you must tell your pupil so. But do not be afraid to tell him also that there are good and holy and scholarly men who think of it as a great old-world allegory, like the parable of the Prodigal Son, to teach in easy popular form profound lessons about sin. Endeavor in your Bible teaching "to be thoroughly truthful: to assert nothing as certain which is not certain, nothing as probable which is not probable, and nothing as more probable than it is." Let the pupil see that there are some things that we cannot be quite sure about, and let him gather insensibly from your teaching the conviction that truth, above all things, is to be loved and sought, and that religion has never anything to fear from discovering the truth. If we could but get this healthy, manly, common-sense attitude adopted now in teaching the Bible to young people, we should, with

God's blessing, have in the new generation a stronger and more intelligent faith.

3. Movere (to move)

All your teaching is useless unless it have this object: to move the heart, to rouse the affections toward the love of God, and the will toward the effort after the blessed life. You interest in order to teach. You teach in order to move. *That* is the supreme object. Here the teacher must be left largely to his own resources. One suggestion I offer: don't preach. At any rate, don't preach much lest you lose grip of your pupils. You have their attention all right while their minds are occupied by a carefully prepared lesson; but wait till you close your Bible, and, assuming a long face, begin, "And now, boys," etc. and straightway they know what is coming, and you have lost them in a moment.

Do not change your tone at the application of your lesson. Try to keep the teaching still conversational. Try still in this more spiritual part of your teaching to question into them what you want them to learn. Appeal to the judgment and to the conscience. I can scarce give a better example than that of our Lord in teaching the parable of the Good Samaritan. He first interested His pupil by putting His lesson in an attractive form, and then He did not append to it a long, tedious moral. He simply asked the man before Him, "Which of these three *thinkest thou?*"—i.e., "What do you think about it?" The interest was still kept up. The man, pleased at the appeal to his judgment, replied promptly, "He that showed mercy on him;" and on the instant came the quick rejoinder, "Go, and do thou likewise." Thus the lesson ends. Try to work on that model.

Now, while forbidding preaching to your pupils, may I be permitted a little preaching myself? This series of lessons is intended for Sunday schools as well as week-day schools. It is of Sunday-school teachers I am thinking in what I am now about to say. I cannot escape the solemn feeling of the responsibility of every teacher for the children in his care. Some of these children have little or no religious influence exerted on them for the whole week except in this one hour with you. Do not make light of this work. Do not get to think, with good-natured optimism, that all the nice, pleasant children in your class are pretty sure to be Christ's soldiers and servants by-and-by. Alas! for the crowds of these nice, pleasant children, who, in later life, wander away from Christ into the ranks of evil. Do not take this danger lightly. Be anxious; be prayerful; be terribly in earnest, that the one hour in the week given you to use be wisely and faithfully used.

But, on the other hand, be very hopeful too, because of the love of God. He will not judge you hardly. Remember that He will bless very feeble work, if it be your best. Remember that He cares infinitely more for the children's welfare than you do, and, therefore, by His grace, much of the teaching about which you are despondent may bring forth good fruit in the days to come. Do you know the lines about "The Noisy Seven"?—

10

"I wonder if he remembers—
    Our sainted teacher in heaven—
The class in the old grey schoolhouse,
    Known as the 'Noisy Seven'?

"I wonder if he remembers
    How restless we used to be.
Or thinks we forget the lesson
    Of Christ and Gethsemane?

"I wish I could tell the story
    As he used to tell it then;
I'm sure that, with Heaven's blessing,
    It would reach the hearts of men.

"I often wish I could tell him,
    Though we caused him so much pain
By our thoughtless, boyish frolic,
    His lessons were not in vain.

"I'd like to tell him how Willie,
    The merriest of us all,
From the field of Balaclava
    Went home at the Master's call.

"I'd like to tell him how Ronald,
    So brimming with mirth and fun,
Now tells the heathen of India
    The tale of the Crucified One.

"I'd like to tell him how Robert,
    And Jamie, and George, and 'Ray,'
Are honoured in the Church of God—
    The foremost men of their day.

"I'd like, yes, I'd like to tell him
    What his lesson did for me;
And how I am trying to follow
    The Christ of Gethsemane.

"Perhaps he knows it already,
    For Willie has told him, maybe,
That we are all coming, coming
    Through Christ of Gethsemane.

"How many besides I know not
    Will gather at last in heaven,
The fruit of that faithful sowing,
    But the sheaves are already seven."

PART I

THE BOOK OF JOSHUA

Lecture to the Teacher

In beginning the study of this Book for the purpose of teaching there are some points which it is important to be clear about.

I

First, that the Book naturally divides itself into two parts:—

The Story of the Conquest, chs. i.-xii.

The Chronicle of the Allotment, chs. xii.-xxiii.

With the Chronicle of the Allotment, or, as it has been called, The Domesday Book of Palestine, our lessons have but little to do. On the Story of the Conquest it may be necessary to make some remarks. Keep clearly in mind that by the Conquest is meant only the conquest of west Palestine. The closing years of Moses were mainly occupied with the subjugation of the fierce tribes on the *eastern* bank of the Jordan. Sihon, King of the Amorites, and Og, the King of

Bashan, and the princes of the wandering Midianites, had fallen before the victorious arms of Israel when our story opens with Joshua and his warriors drawn up on the banks of the Jordan. It is entirely with the conquest of West Palestine—ie., Palestine beyond the Jordan—Palestine between the Jordan and the Mediterranean Sea—that we are concerned in this Book. Show this to the class by means of the map. Be careful, too, to avoid the common misapprehension that Joshua's conquest was a complete one—a misapprehension which causes a good deal of puzzling about the condition of things at the opening of the Book of Judges. From ch. xv. 63, xvi. 10, xvii. 12, 13, etc., it is clear that portions of the subjugated tribes remained, pretty much like the ancient Britons in England long ago, holding the fastnesses, and sometimes permitted to dwell with the conquerors and pay tribute, and that these were a serious danger and temptation to the Israelites. We shall find in the Book of Judges that the Israelites were themselves to blame for this; but the matter does not further concern us in this Book.

II

Let us next try to form an opinion about those Canaanite tribes which were driven out by the children of Israel. They are named in different parts of the Bible the Canaanites, Amorites, Hittites, Perizzites, Hivites, Jebusites, Gergashites; but they seem to have had the same language, and manners, and religious customs,

14

and are frequently spoken of under the general name of Canaanites or Hittites.

The Bible tells us very little of their history, and very little of their manners, beyond the terrible statements as to their cruelty and impurity, and the unutterable abominations connected with their heathen worship. The very earth itself beneath their feet is represented as unable to bear their filthy and licentious lives. Their sand is said to vomit them forth (Leviticus xviii. 25). But secular history throws a new light on them rather startling at first sight. We have heard of Cadmus, the Phœnician, the inventor of the alphabet; of the Phœnician ships that traded for tin with early Britain; of the Phœnician race the pioneers of commerce—who colonized the Mediterranean shores. We know something of that most interesting period in Roman history which tells of the power and civilization of Carthage, and the wars of its Punic or Phœnician race—the great merchant princes of the world. Is it not startling to discover that the polished Phœnician and the accursed Canaanite are one and the same! The Septuagint translators of the Old Testament actually use the word "Phœnician" in translating the Hebrew term "Canaanite" (Exodus xvi. 35; Joshua v. 1). St Augustine, in his Commentary of the Epistle to the Romans, says that the country folk around Carthage called themselves Canaani. And many teachers will remember the Carthaginian names— Hannibal, Asdrubal, Maherbal, with the title Baal at the end, recalling the dark idol of the Israelite days, and the names Eshbaal and Merib-baal, even among the children of Saul.

Apart from the interest of the fact that we can identify the Canaanite with the famous Phœnician, there is an instructive lesson here for our senior classes. It is quite true that at this period the Phœnician race had passed its zenith of greatness, and was probably advancing toward demoralization and decay. We know they had not always been so wicked and depraved. There was a time when their "iniquity was not yet full." Yet, even so, there is a lesson in the difference of attitude of the sacred and secular historians, "The Lord seeth not as man seeth. Man looketh on the outward appearance, but the Lord looketh on the heart." Power, civilization, knowledge, beauty, win the admiration of the careless world even when covering a mass of moral corruption. With God the chief thing is the *man himself*—the moral nature within. According as that is turned to the true and noble, or the base and sensual, so are men and nations judged by God. Probably much of the graceful and beautiful in our notions of ancient Greek life would similarly vanish at the Ithuriel touch of an inspired historian, and appear, it may be, in the lurid colours of St. Paul's first chapter in his Epistle to the Romans.

III

The miracles in this Book of Joshua have often raised doubts and disturbance in men's minds. That the waters of Jordan should part for their crossing—that the walls of the city of Jericho should fall to the ground—are events that would *in ordinary circumstances* seem so improbable that a man feels half justified in hesitating to believe them. But be it remembered *that these were not ordinary circumstances.* What was at stake was not, as sceptics sneeringly assert, the fate of a few thousand Jews, or the "mastership of a little province about the size of Wales"—no, but the fate of the Torch-bearers who were to bear the light of the truth for the whole human race. The issue of the conquest of Palestine belongs to all time. The Jews were a people miraculously used for the sake of humanity. Their history must be read, as the historian wrote it, with an awful sense of God's immediate presence pervading it right through. We feel no difficulty about miracles in the days of the Apostles. We feel that they are extraordinary, but that they are for an extraordinary time. Let the same thought have place in reading about this period.

This does not mean that we must accept each statement unquestioningly as an exact literal explanation of what actually happened. Something wonderful *did* happen at the Jordan and at Jericho which made a tremendous impression. Here is no questioning of miracles, of what God *could* have done. But some accounts may strike us as improbable as to what God *would* have done. It is not wrong to think of other possible explanations. The stories of these miracles are not as regards evidence on the level of those recorded in our Lord's day. They belong to far remote antiquity. They came down for generations in the legends of the people. We must allow for the possibility of exaggeration and poetical expression. But there is no escaping the conviction that the whole period was felt by the actors in it to be a time of the extraordinary and supernatural.

God was very near to them. We find the statement that the natives were terrified at the invaders as men helped supernaturally, so that all "hearts did melt, neither did there remain any more courage in any man because of them." We find the simple, artless historian before us fearlessly appealing to the monuments existing, he says, "even to this day" in which he wrote. He never seems to have troubled himself about proving or persuading—he seems to have never a thought of anyone questioning his story. Simply and straightforwardly he tells his tale, utterly unconscious of what seem difficulties to us. And, what is a much more important fact, we find the whole subsequent history and prophecies and psalms of the nation deeply stamped with the memory of this miraculous time. The existence of the miraculous is the only explanation. It will be noticed that I have not here included the mention of the sun standing still. What I have just said about the miracles of the Book does not equally apply to this, so I leave it for separate treatment in its appointed place in the Lessons.

IV

There is no room in this brief note to do more than touch the main difficulty of the Book—the slaughter of the Canaanites.

First of all, get rid of the thought of FAVOURITISM, which underlies much of the difficulty. The Israelites were not pets and favourites chosen arbitrarily for their own sakes to a favoured life. They were a race elected to great responsibilities and terribly severe training, *not for their own sakes, but for the sake of humanity.* The Israelites were the trustees of religion and morality for the whole world. If they had lost their sacred deposit in the abominations of Canaan, the whole human race might have sunk to the level of Sodom. They were used to punish terribly the unutterable abominations of Canaan; but they were punished as terribly themselves when they committed the same abominations. Nothing could impress the horror and hatefulness of sin so strongly on the Israelites as the solemn experiences of this early period in their history. They were taught to look on themselves as God's executioners performing a judicial act in His name. It was that which saved them from the brutalizing effect that their destruction of the Canaanites must otherwise have produced. If we are to understand their history we must never think of them as mere marauding tribes going forth to win land and booty for themselves. They were God's crusaders consecrated to an awful mission. Other nations have gone out to fight for their own glory or for increase of territory. "There is one nation which is taught from the first that it is not to go out to win any prizes for itself, to bring home the silver or gold, the sheep or the oxen; that it is simply the instrument of the righteous Lord against those who were polluting His earth and making it unfit for human habitation." The awful catalogue of abominations, too horrible to read in Leviticus xviii. to xx. are distinctly said to have been those committed by the men of the land so that the land was defiled therewith and that God abhorred it.

All this does not make it necessary for you to justify

to yourself the whole attitude of the Israelites to the people of Canaan, or to think that it would be the fitting attitude for Christian men in the same circumstances now. You must remember God's *gradual progressive education* of humanity. Think of the world as God's great school, with its gradual training, and these Israelites as His early scholars in the lower classes of that school. The religion of the Old Testament days, noble though it was, was far lower than the religion taught to us by Christ. He clearly lays down the difference Himself. (see Matthew v. 17, 21, 27, 33, 38, 43.) These Israelites were in the lower stages of the Divine teaching. They had learned to hate sin with a great hatred; but they had not learned to distinguish between sin and the sinner. Even in the Psalms, with their lofty moral teachings and aspirations after God and holiness, we are frequently startled by the fierce prayers for punishment on the wicked. They are the prayers of stern, faithful servants of God, claiming that He should vindicate His justice. But they belong to an age when moral indignation against evil showed itself in invoking vengeance on the evil-doer as the enemy of God. That was the important element in Israel's religion—a very important element, indeed, in all men's religion—fierce indignation against moral evil—against oppression, and impurity, and idolatry, and wrong of every kind. It was a grand religion for a lower, rougher, fiercer age than ours. The Gospel added to it the duty of distinguishing between the sin and the sinner. But be it remembered that that Gospel teaching was of later date. Keep that fact in mind. Try to put yourself in the place of the stern Israelite leaders, feeling themselves as the agent of Jehovah to sweep oppression and impurity from the earth. Try to keep in mind the Bible accounts of the awful abominations of Canaan. Not many years ago, England was sending out soldiers to Benin, to punish and, if necessary, destroy, an utterly abominable race; and the English newspapers were loudly praising the object of the expedition. Many good people had the same feeling with regard to the Turks, as the accounts came in of the Armenian massacres. During the Indian Mutiny it is recorded that an officer wrote home: "The Book of Joshua is now being read in the Church Lessons. It expresses exactly what we are feeling. I never before understood the force of that part of the Bible."

Let such things help us to understand the position of faithful men in ancient Israel, with God's inspiration of righteousness stirring in their souls. Let us remember that the fuller teaching of Christ was not theirs; "Many prophets and righteous men have not seen them, and to hear the things which ye hear, and have not heard them."

Above all, impress on yourself and on your class the conviction which you have learned from the whole Bible, and especially from the New Testament, that the Judge of all the earth must do right. Therefore, even if there be no record to convince you of it in the present history, be sure that there is no unfairness with God. If there was unfairness or cruelty in the half savage Israelites, it need not surprise us if we realize their low moral stage at the time. Nor even that they should believe such to be the will of God. Then believe in God's patience.

Four hundred years God had waited, "for the iniquity of the Amorites is not yet full." (Genesis xv. 16). He had waited to see if they would do better. He had helped them to do so. We find one great Canaanite teacher at least, Melchizedek, priest of the Most High God, and we know not how many successors he may have had, and who were sent in God's good Providence to help the people. Perhaps, in later days, too, God had given them teachers, as to other heathen nations, like Jethro or Balaam or like Jonah in Nineveh or like Gautama Buddha in India. He had certainly helped them by His "law written in their hearts, their conscience bearing witness." (Romans ii. 15). In all nations we find the stirrings of conscience and the dim yearning for better things. And the Bible (e.g., John i. 9, Acts xvii. 23, 26, 27) fully confirms the beautiful creed of Longfellow:—

> "That in even savage bosoms
> There are longings, yearnings, strivings,
> For the good they comprehend not;
> And the feeble hands and helpless,
> Groping blindly in the darkness,
> Touch God's right hand in that darkness,
> And are lifted up and strengthened."
> —*Hiawatha.*

We know little about the Canaanites and their "fair chance" in this life. But we may rest in the firm belief that God condemns no man without his "fair chance." When you shrink from the thought of these Canaanites with their little and their great sins, being cut off suddenly, men and women and even little children, do not assume hastily that that must inevitably mean for all of them eternal damnation. Remember that, after death, as before death, men are still in the hands of the same just loving God who "willeth all men to be saved." Remember that the Canaanites are waiting still in the great Hades life for the final judgment at the coming of the Son of Man. They are not yet judged, not yet finally condemned. And as you think of the indication given us (1 Peter iii. 19, 20; iv. 6) of that Son of Man appearing in the Hades life to preach the "good news" to them that were dead of the antediluvian world, why should you not hope the same thing for the Canaanites if they had no fair chance on earth of knowing God? True we can only guess at the mysteries of the Unseen Life. But we can know with positive certainty that "the Judge of all the earth will do right."

Be sure then that neither the heathen of Canaan in olden days, nor the heathen of India and China to-day, have any unfair treatment meted out to them by God. The real cure for Old Testament difficulties, as for all the difficulties of life, is this:—HAVE FAITH IN GOD. Faith in God means faith in a Person, faith in a character, faith in an infinite love and nobleness, generosity and unselfishness—faith in One to whom it would be absolutely impossible that He should be unfair, or ungenerous, or unkind to any man. Learn that faith yourself. Resolve, God helping you, to teach that faith to your class, and, if you do nothing more, your work in that class will be well worth the doing.

THE SECRET OF COURAGE

Joshua I.

§ 1. *Introduction*

Have you ever read the story, *From Log Cabin to White House?* It tells how a little peasant lad became President of the United States. Or the story of *The Slave Boy Who Became a Bishop?* (Bishop Crowther, of the Niger Mission, in Africa.)

Our story to-day tells of a slave boy (in Africa also) who became a great commander. Who? When slave boy, and where? Yes. At the time when Moses began to take slaves' part, when he killed the Egyptian oppressor, and fled for his life, Joshua was but a little baby—the child of slaves. Grew up a slave. Probably often flogged by overseers, or saw his parents flogged at the brick kiln. But don't you think a man may be a splendid fellow even if a slave? I think Joshua was. I want you really to know him, and get interested in him, for he well deserves it, as we shall see in these lessons. For when Moses led out Israel, Joshua was with him as his lieutenant. He was so thoroughly faithful to God and to duty—so true, brave, candid, unselfish. No wonder Moses grew so attached to him, made him his friend. As he grew older he liked to have the young man about him—sent him on great expeditions. What? To fight with Amalek (Exodus xvii. 9); to spy out the Promised Land. Remember the anger of people with Joshua that day. How grandly he spoke to them to rouse their courage (Numbers xiv.). He was a great help to Moses. He knew most of the old leader's thoughts, and cares, and troubles. Had gone up with him for the Tables of the Law. Had seen him break them in anger at the peoples' sin. Had seen how those people worried and fretted him, rebelled against him, almost stoned him (Exodus xvii. 4), and at last how they irritated him so much that he lost all patience, and sinned—how? Sad punishment inflicted by God. What? He must never enter the Land, must die in the wilderness. Up the lonely mountain he passed from the view of the people, and there he died—alone—with God.

Now we turn to to-day's lesson. Great camp of Israel on plains of Moab.

§ 2. God Always Remains

Now the days of sorrow and wailing in the camp upon the plains of Moab. Why? Moses is dead. Their father, and friend, and leader. The captain who had fought for them. The prophet who had prayed for them. Don't you think they would be sorry now for the past? Why? Frightened about the future? Why? The most dangerous part of their journey yet to be done. How frightened and hopeless! The great hero gone—the only hero they had ever known. Surely no one could supply his place. Was it a natural feeling? Was it right? Why not? What were they forgetting? Though Moses was gone, who always remained?

People often frightened thus when great men died, in the nation—in the Church (give examples). What should they remember? God always there. God "buries His workers, but carries on His work." (See Lessons on Genesis, last chapter.) Is this only true in Bible history? Is it in American history? *E.g.,* The Church—Missionary work, Suppression of slave trade, etc. Difference between American history and Bible history? Is God behind both—managing both? The chief difference is that the Jewish historians were inspired, and could recognize God in all; the English historian sometimes cannot see Him. But He is there all the same.

Had God forgotten to have new leader ready? Whom? Look back and see preparation. People call these things chance till they see whole view. Little boy born while Moses fretted in Midian. Grew up an earnest, religious man. Was it all chance? Tell me more of his preparation. Became dear to Moses, was taught and trusted by him in difficult affairs. Was it chance? Sent to lead the troops—to spy out the Land—just the right training for a leader. Was this chance? At any rate the result of all these "chances" was that when the old leader was struck down with the most critical part of his work left undone, a man was waiting, ready, trained, to whom the solemn charge of God could come:—"Moses, my servant is dead; now therefore arise, go over this Jordan, thou, and all this people." Ah! these things are not chance in Joshua's days or in ours. God's plan. So John Baptist, St. Paul, Luther, etc. So, too, with much less important people, God has a plan for us all.

§ 3. *The Secret of Courage*

Now tell me God's command to Joshua (*v.* 2). Do you think Joshua would take it up with light heart without fear or unwillingness? Were they easy, pleasant people to lead? He knew their rebellion and grumbling, how they had nearly broken Moses' heart. He knew the awful task before him. Was it easier than Moses'? Harder? Why? Not only lead, but lead in constant battle against powerful enemies—against trained soldiers—great cities—Israelites not able for them, rebellious, weak, often cowardly—slave blood in them, etc. *(Expand and emphasize these difficulties.)* Might it not well frighten any leader?

Was Joshua frightened? No (*vv.* 10, 11). How did he dare to undertake it? By FAITH! Faith in God—and Right—and Duty. What was God's promise? (*v.* 5). Yes. He felt God would be with him—the work was laid on him by God. God was responsible for him, and would see him through with it. Suppose I ordered this class to start for Central Africa to-morrow, to pass through black warriors, and give message to black king, could you do it? Why? No money, no knowledge of country, no protection, etc., no chance of seeing black king. But suppose the President sent you? What a difference it

27

would make. He would be responsible for you, supply your wants, protect you. What matter the danger and difficulty with the power of your nation at your back?

That was Joshua's feeling. What if Canaanites were giants! What if the people rebelled! What if he should be fretted and disappointed? What if he should be killed before Jericho! What matter? It was God's affair. God was responsible for him in life and in death. What was God's command? (*vv.* 6, 7). What is it in all the struggles of life that makes men strong and courageous? Faith in God and in Duty, which comes from God. What will make your life and mine strong, peaceful, brave? To know that God is with you—standing on your side. When can you be sure of that? When, like Joshua, you are in the path of duty, wanting and trying to do His will. Then your spirit can hear the words that Joshua heard:—"Be strong and of good courage," etc. (repeat *v.* 9). You are even better off than Joshua; you have a grander revelation of God. Joshua did not know all the love of God and His care for men as the Lord Jesus has taught them to us.

QUESTIONS FOR LESSON I

Show on map west Palestine where this story belongs.

Who was to lead Israel after Moses' death?

What training had he had? Find some instances.

"God buries His workers but carries on His work." Explain and give instance.

Repeat God's encouragement to Joshua, "Be strong," etc.

What promise of God would make him strong and courageous? (*v.* 5).

How are we in this matter even better off than Joshua?

LESSON II

GOD'S POWER

Joshua III.

Recapitulate. What was Joshua's chief characteristic? Courage. What will do most to make our lives courageous? Remember illustration last lesson of your being sent to Africa. Repeat it. That was Joshua's faith.

Now comes a test of this faith in God. What? They knew that the river Jordan in high flood (*v.* 15) had to be crossed. No bridge. Dangerous, impossible to attempt marching through a deep river with an enemy watching to swoop down on them at the crossing. Did Joshua give up? Not he! He had been commanded to march on. But the people surely were puzzled and afraid. "How can we? We shall surely be stopped when we come to the river."

People are often like that still when they see a duty before them and it seems impossible to do it. What should they do? If it be clearly a duty which they feel God wants done better go straight ahead and try it at any rate and leave result with God. People are often frightened unnecessarily at difficulties which vanish when they come up to them. *E.g.,* the women going to tomb of Jesus on Easter morning. Who shall roll us away the stone? Women could not attempt to move the great rock at door of tomb. What happened? When they came they found the stone had been rolled away. So they had been worrying unnecessarily. Just like that here.

Joshua knew that God would make it possible for them. What did he command? (*v.* 5). Sanctify yourselves. Why? How? Clothes washed and pure. God taught them like children by object-lessons. Must be clean and pure drawing near to God's presence. Sanctify their hearts too in preparation—examine themselves about the past, repent of all wrong, resolve henceforth to serve God better. Just like people before Holy Communion.

So they came to the banks of the Jordan all frightened, excited. Then with astonishment and awe and gratitude in their hearts they saw—what? The river went dry before their eyes. Somewhere far back the river stopped flowing and the lower waters flowed away to the sea, leaving a dry river bed for the people to cross! How could the river stop flowing? By a miracle from God. Perhaps God did it by what would seem to us a natural occurrence. It has been suggested that somewhere far back was a narrow gorge of the river and that a great landslide fell in there and stopped the river for hours. It is interesting here to notice that there is a record by an Arabic chronicler telling of the sudden damming of the Jordan by a landslide in A.D. 1267. (See Hasting's *Dictionary of Bible,* article Joshua.) Maybe something like that happened here. If so would it be less a miracle of God? Why? Because a landslide happening just at the critical moment is as miraculous as any other miracle. For example, in 1588, when the great Spanish Armada was about to crush England, and the people in their dread were calling upon God—just in the crisis of their danger a great storm came that blew the Spanish fleet irresistibly northward and ruined their whole expedition. A storm was quite a natural thing, but the English people looked on it as an answer to their prayers and lifted up their hearts to God in thanksgiving for a great deliverance.

We do not at all know that there was a landslide at the Jordan. We are only guessing. We only know the belief of the people as told us in the book that the waters far above were stopped and the waters below flowed on to the sea. And that Joshua and his people bowed with wonder and gratitude before God and set up a memorial (*ch.* iv.), a caisson of great stones from the Jordan piled up at the crossing place where God had done this mighty deed for Israel, and that the Canaanites heard that the Lord had dried up Jordan before the feet of the children of Israel and their hearts melted, neither was there spirit in them any more because of the children of Israel (*ch.* v. 1).

Now what do we learn from this story? Let the class guess the answers, and then emphasize for them these two:—

(1) That God is what Joshua called Him, "the living God," "the Lord of all the earth," master of all the powers of nature, ruler of all the nations of the earth. That He is looking down still on all peoples, the Friend of all righteousness, the enemy of all evil. That in the recent Great War He was looking down and caring and listening to prayers as in the days of Israel and the Canaanites. He is still the living ruling God.

(2) That no matter what obstacles are in the path of a duty, if we are sure it is God's will then that makes it God's command and we must go straight ahead like Joshua and trust Him and leave results to Him. Deal especially with the duties and difficulties likely to come to your pupils. Then close with the thought that God's presence is as sure to us as it was to Joshua. He can lead us through all struggles—through all human opposition and at the end of the life battle lead us across the Jordan of death into the Promised Land beyond.

QUESTIONS FOR LESSON II

What was the first test of faith of Joshua and his host?

What religious direction did he give the people before coming to Jordan?

What did they find when they came to the river?

Tell of instance in secular history somewhat like this.

If it happened through a landslide would it be less a miracle? Why?

What lesson here about God?

What lesson about duty?

LESSON III

JERICHO

Joshua V. v. 10 to end, and VI.

Get through the repetition of other lessons quickly to-day, to give more time. This Lesson has to be a little longer than usual, owing to the necessity for Section 1.

Now we are approaching delicate ground—the subject of the wars with Canaan. Be very careful that you do not "lie for God" or place burdens on the consciences of your class by making them say words of approval, and yet letting them think in their hearts that the Canaanites were harshly or unfairly treated for the sake of God's favourites, the Jews. They may do this without your knowing it if you are not watchful. The destruction of the Canaanites is a hard subject to bring before children. If possible, one would rather omit it till they were older. If you don't feel quite clear about the matter yourself, do not dwell upon it much. But in any case do not overthrow the authority of conscience in the pupil, or set God's acts in opposition to conscience.

Insist on the point in Section 1, that the Judge of all the earth must do right, and that if it seem otherwise to us, it must be because we don't know all the facts. Never let anyone be taught that he must believe of God that from which his conscience shrinks.

Question rapidly about crossing of Jordan in last Lesson. Its effect on Israel? On Canaanites? (*ch.* v. 1, vi. 1). Now, what next? Fight? No, a great religious ceremony. Never mind enemy or danger. Stop and think of God. Circumcise all the desert-born children. Let the whole nation partake of the Passover. As if it should be said to us: "Let all the unbaptized be baptized. Let the whole nation, hundreds of thousands, kneel down and receive of the Holy Communion." Why did not the enemy attack them while thus engaged? Awe of the supernatural. What a wonderful and solemn sight: the great sacramental consecration of Israel. (If there is time in elder classes, dwell on the great privilege of Holy Communion to which they will soon be admitted. The solemnity of it, the power it brings into life. Tell them of the Christian ideal of a life lived close to Christ by faith and renewed and fed and strengthened week by week or month by month by the regular receiving of the Holy Sacrament, after due preparation.)

§ 1. God's Justice

With this solemn sacramental preparation the work of conquest begins. These nations in their abominable filthy wickedness must be cast out. God had borne with them 400 years. Why? (See Genesis xv. 16.) The iniquity is now full. Had God given them a fair chance? Had God waited to see if they would do better? Probably had raised up teachers among them, like Jethro or Balaam, like Jonah in Nineveh, or Job in Arabia. In any case, we may be sure that He helped them by His Spirit, if they would only obey.

How do we know? (1) Because there is no man in the world not helped by Him. (John i. 9). (2) Because we know how patiently God waited. (Genesis xv. 16). (3) We know that God, just because He is God, *must* act fairly to all men, and give them every chance. The Judge of all the earth will always do right. (Genesis xviii. 25). He could not do otherwise. Therefore, even though it be not told us, we know that these heathen and all heathen are helped, though not with the full gift of the Holy Ghost won for us by Christ. Does God demand as much from them as from us? But He demands *some* efforts after right. They have conscience to help them. (Romans ii. 15). They have, as it were, the outer skirts of the Holy Spirit's robe touching them, rousing in them the desire for right and remorse for wrong. So that we may rest satisfied that God was not unfair to the Canaanites. It seems to have been absolutely necessary to destroy them, else they would corrupt Israel, who were to teach and hand down God's religion to the whole world—so the whole human race would be injured. But though destroyed in this life, this life is a small matter in God's sight. He had all the life of eternity still to help these Canaanites.

§ 2. The Captain of the Lord's Host

Now we resume our story. Picture the great crowds waiting and resting in the fields by the river, praying to God, preparing for the holy Passover feast. Joshua has moved away alone. He is in deep thought. The mighty stronghold of Jericho lies before him, with its high, strong walls and towers, and its trained soldiers to guard it. He is examining its defenses, trying to make plans for assaulting it.

It must be taken somehow, for it guards the only two passes through the mountains into the country. (Make a rough sketch on paper of two passes and a fortress in front.) The Israelites have the river behind them and the fortress before them. They must conquer or be lost. The general is in deep thought. He is responsible for that crowd of people. Do you think he is anxious, uneasy? Why? Because he knows and trusts God too well. How can he doubt Him after the crossing of Jordan? Suddenly, as he walks he feels a presence near him. He lifts up his eyes and sees. What? Describe Him. Repeatedly all through the Bible we have visitants from the spirit world doing God's will, bearing God's messages. That spirit world seems a very kindly, friendly world deeply interested in our world here. Tell me of some such appearances in our Lord's time.

What was his title here? What was "the Lord's host"? The host of the angels of God. (There was a curious story in the Great War of a white angel host at Mons coming to help at a terrible crisis. It was repeated by many who claimed to have seen them. I know nothing about the truth of it.) He leads the heavenly host in the great conflict with the foes of God and man. This host would be marching invisible with the Israelites as they walked around the walls of Jericho. The people had but to walk round, and shout, and blow their trumpets; the invisible host of God would throw down the walls. We have reason to believe that they, too, are around us always, ministering and helping. (Hebrews i. 14). Remember Elisha's servants (2 Kings vi. 17), whose eyes were opened to see them. Perhaps if our spiritual eyes were opened to-day, we should be rather startled to find that we are not nearly so much alone as we think.

§ 3. The Fall of Jericho

The great siege has begun! The strangest siege ever seen in the world. Imagine the men of Jericho crowded on the walls waiting for the attack. Ah, it is coming! Tramp, tramp, hear the steady step of soldiers. See the armed men of Israel marching toward the wall. "Now they are going to attack!" No! What does it mean? Steadily, silently they pass on round the walls, and behind them are seven priests with trumpets of ram's horns, and behind them that awful, mysterious thing, the ark of God, which the Canaanites had already seen in front of procession across Jordan—when the waters shrank away before it. Then, behind all, the main body of the people.

Tramp, tramp, steadily round—every man grimly silent. No shouting or cheering. No noise of battle. Silence, solemn, awful silence everywhere. And now they have finished the round, and away they march back to camp. Wondering and fearing, these men of Jericho wait and watch all night. Next day the same mysterious movements, and next day and every day for a week, still silent, awfully, terribly silent. What could it all mean? Do you think Jericho men wondered? Do you think they were amused? Ah, no! That awful ark terrified them. They knew the Israelites would not dare to do this without good reason. They could have sallied out on the defenseless procession behind the ark, but they dared not. They knew something of the mysterious story of this people. They knew that this silent, awful march of soldiers who did not attack—this procession with the ark, and the priests, and the awe-struck multitude behind, meant something very solemn. Then at last on the seventh day there was a change. Very early the awful procession came. Round and round it went—once? No, but seven times. Suddenly there was a pause. Then in a moment the awful silence was broken by the sharp, ringing sound of the horns, and the mighty cry of a great multitude shouting together. And higher, louder, more awful than all came the terrible crash of walls and towers, and the cry of a great crowd of people crushed beneath the fall. And when the Israelites could see through the falling stones and dust, behold, Jericho was overthrown. The walls were lying flat on the ground. Perhaps the invisible army, the mighty angels of the Lord's host, had touched the walls, and they fell down flat. We know nothing further about it. We simply read the mysterious story in this ancient book. We know of mysterious powers revealed by modern science. We know of men by touching an electric button bringing down great walls and towers. And we know all things are possible with God. We can say no more about it.

§ 4. The Lesson

(a) *God sets us, also, tasks impossible to ourselves alone.* What tasks? To enter the strait gate, to live the Christ-life, to "keep His holy will and commandments, and walk in the same all the days of our life." Are they not as utterly impossible as the taking of Jericho?

(b) *How do we succeed? By Faith.* By faith the Israelites walked round Jericho. "By faith the walls of Jericho fell down." (Hebrews xi. 30). What was their faith? Their faith was *not mere belief.* They had to risk and dare much for it. They trusted God's word, and therefore they walked round quietly, though apparently in great danger from the Canaanites. So with us. Faith is far more than merely believing something. Believing comes first. Believing that God will forgive, will help. Believing that He cares for our spiritual victory more than we care ourselves. And then—what? Struggle, and risk, and dare everything for what we know is God's will—that is faith. And He will always honour that faith, and enable us to conquer.

QUESTIONS FOR LESSON III

What was the object of the great religious ceremony after crossing the Jordan?

Who were the Canaanites?

What character?

What famous people in Roman history were Canaanites?

What do you know of "the Captain of the Lord's host"?

What other instances in Scripture of beings from the other world appearing to men?

Tell of the fall of Jericho.

ACHAN—THE DECEITFULNESS OF SIN

Joshua VII.

Try to fix the interest on Achan from the beginning. The external scene is not as important to bring before the pupils as the feelings of Achan. Try to "put yourself in his place." Try to make class realize the treacherous nature of sin. How it entices, and promises, and lulls into security. Teach them:—This is one of your enemy's wiles. As Christ's soldier you must learn this to help your warfare. In senior classes show how shame and loss is brought on a whole parish or association by one member. How the work of a parish for God may be a failure through the bad influence of one or two.

Remember importance of capture of Jericho. Key to the passes behind. Would not Israelites now be confident? Exultant? Trustful? Flushed with victory, they would sweep all before them. First expedition against what town? How prepared for? Advice of spies?

§ 1. Israel's Reverse

Now picture the start. Great camp round ruins of Jericho. All the people in thousands watching the warriors start. Only three thousand—but quite enough. God with Israel—victory assured. Watch the three thousand steadily filing through the mountain passes—lost sight of—people waiting all day and next day to welcome the victors with rejoicings. Morning—midday—evening passed—victors not yet coming. Now at last the shout—"Here they come!" See the gleam of the spears upon the hillside! Nearer, nearer, hasten out to meet them! But stop! No joyous trumpets nor shouts of victory. See how they are straggling—how dejected and weary. Surely this is not the march of victorious troops. Soon the news spread. Oh, horror and shame! They return defeated—have fled for their lives—thirty-six of their comrades left dead upon the battle-field. What was the effect on Israel? (*v.* 5). In a critical position now. Just like the time long ago when they had almost got into Palestine before, and were repulsed at Hormah, and turned back for forty years. Is this to be the end? "Has God given us up?" Did Joshua feel it much? Did the other chiefs? How show it? (*v.* 6). To whom did they flee in their trouble? What did Joshua say? Do you think he lost faith? Yes, for the time. Even Joshua only human. For the moment all his brave trust gone. "O God, why did You bring us over Jordan to deliver us to our enemies? We are ruined—we are disgraced for ever." Anything to blame in Joshua's attitude? What? Anything to praise? (a) That he fled to God at once, like a big child running to his father with every trouble.

(b) It was not any selfish cry. It was for his people's sake and for God's honour.

§ 2. The Sin

Was Joshua right in his doubts of God? What was God's answer? Yes. "I have not changed. I am not unfaithful to My people; but they have sinned, and therefore cannot conquer. Put away the sin, and let the transgressor suffer, and sanctify the people, and then ye shall conquer." What an impression this would make! What new hopes would rise! Imagine the defeated warriors looking at each other. "Ah! it was some sin amongst us that made us weak. Who could it have been? How can we find out?" Imagine the clamour, and the talking, and the wonder, and the secret suspicions of each other. What was the method appointed for the discovery? Did you ever see lots drawn? Give any example—*e.g.,* hold slips of paper of different lengths in hand, and let pupils draw, and see who gets shortest. Would this plan find out a thief to-day? No. Explain: God would guide. Remember another instance? (Acts i. 26). Imagine the excitement of that night, as they watched for the early morning when the great public trial should be! Imagine the terror of one man—whom? Do you think he slept much that night?

§ 3. The Discovery

All bustle and excitement—trumpets sound, warriors march out—separate according to tribes—Simeon here, Reuben there. Judah on this side—so on. Now, which tribe was Achan in? Keep your eye on tribe of Judah. Dead silence. First lot about to be drawn. Oh, if some other tribe should be drawn, what a relief to Achan! See the drawing. Hear the trumpet. Now it is announced—JUDAH! The other tribes all fall back with great feeling of relief. Judah stands alone. One man trying to look unconcerned, but trembling with terror. Silence again—the people hardly breathe as they listen. ZARHITES! Watch Achan now! The men of his family are ordered to stand out, and all the rest of Judah retire. Now the last lot. Which man of the Zarhites? Achan knows well what is coming—he feels the terrible circle of God's search getting narrower and narrower. How awful God is when a man is hiding sin! Ah! the lot is drawn. The herald calls out the name. What? ACHAN! Oh, poor miserable Achan, that thought to deceive God! There he stands now alone with his conscience— alone with his shame and fear, before the crowd of warriors defeated through him—before the widows and orphans of the dead soldiers who lie outside Ai. All his fault, poor stricken, guilty wretch. He must confess now. Can't hide any longer. What had he done? (*v.* 21). Where hidden? Messengers bring spoils, and lay them out before the Lord. Think of Achan's misery. Think of the awful punishment in the valley of Achor, where he and his family all were publicly executed, as an awful lesson to Israel about the hatefulness of sin.

§ 4. *The Lesson: The Deceitfulness of Sin*

1. *As to its pleasantness.* Now tell me, was it worth all this punishment? Is sin ever worth it? Think of any sin done by you, and then think of Achan's sin. Why did he commit it? Thought it would be pleasant. Just what everyone thinks beforehand. But think of his fear of discovery—fear about his hiding-place—fear of taking it out to use it. Think of his conscience and his fear of God. Think of the thirty-six dead comrades whose death is on his soul. Altogether, don't you think the pleasure would be rather spoiled? That is the curse of all sin. It seems pleasant before it is done; then it is bitter and disagreeable. Like the fabled Dead Sea fruit, lovely to look at, which turns to dust and ashes on the lips. God has put that curse on sin, it is so hateful in His sight.

2. *As to its secrecy.* "Tush, God does not see it!" Is that true? Sees everything. And he has made conscience awfully powerful in lashing us for it. Make them realize the operation of conscience. What an awful witness of God in you when you sin! (1) Conscience says you ought not. (2) Then it condemns you. (3) Then it threatens you. (4) Then it points away out into the hereafter, and frightens you as to what God will do with the impenitent sinner. (5) The chief part of the agony in the hereafter is probably made by conscience. Here is a man's dream:—

"I sat alone with my conscience in the land where time
     had ceased,
And discoursed of my former living on the earth where
     the years increased;
And I felt I should have to answer the questions it put to me,
And to face those questions and answers through all eternity,
And the ghosts of forgotten actions came floating before
     my sight,
And things that I thought were dead things were alive with
     a terrible might,
And the vision of all my past life was an awful thing to face,
Alone, alone with my conscience, in that dark and
     lonely place.
And I thought of my former thinking of a Judgment
     yet to be;
But my darkest thoughts were far behind the dread reality.

. . . .

And I know of that future Judgment, how awful soe'er it be,
That to sit alone with my conscience would be judgment
     enough for me."

Even if there were no hereafter, would it be worth while choosing a life of sin? What is the one hope and refuge against this treacherous, horrible sin, and the pain of conscience and the displeasure of God? Flee to Christ for help. You are His soldier and servant by baptism. He is bound to stand by you if you cry to Him. Watch the first beginnings of sin. Don't let bad habit get formed. Christ is a thousand times stronger than sin, and He longs to help you, and strengthen you, and make you a glad, holy, faithful Christian. Never lose heart. Confess the sin, and put it away, and God will be then always on your side.

QUESTIONS FOR LESSON IV

Tell of the first startling defeat of Joshua's men.

How did they all feel about it?

What did they find out was the cause?

Tell the way in which they found out.

Name of the man who had here sinned?

What had he done?

Why were Israelites forbidden to take booty?

How is Achan's story like that of Conscience in us when we have done wrong?

What should we do when we have done wrong?

LESSON V

GIBEON

Joshua IX.

Remember how Achan's sin caused defeat. When sin was put away, they returned again to the assault, and utterly destroyed Ai. This, following closely on fall of Jericho, struck renewed terror into the hearts of the neighbouring kings in hill country. Surely their turn next! What did they determine? One city planned otherwise? See Gibeon on map, opposite the pass at Ai; would have been next to fall, could not have been ready to fight in so short a time against such terrible foes. Imagine the chiefs of the town coming together in their fright. Imagine the clamour of the debate. Imagine a crafty old Gibeonite breaking in on the debate with this wily suggestion. Just the thing to delight the wily Orientals. To this day deceit and craft are their strong points. Imagine the doubts and the shaking of heads at the fear of detection. At least it is resolved to try it. People intensely anxious. Will it succeed? Is not the God of these Israelites too wise?

§ 1. The Treaty Made

Now a great hunt through the town for old clothes, old boots, old sacks, old wine-skins, and mouldy bread. Must have enjoyed the mischief of it if they were not too frightened. Next morning they start. Only twenty miles to go. Ever see children pretending to be old—or sick—or lame? Good fun, laughter, amusement. But it was too serious for laughter here. They get the old clothes and clouted boots on—gather up the mouldy bread. Eat a good meal of fresh food before starting, and off they go.

Towards night draw near to Israelite camp. Early next day Israelites look out, and see such a shabby, disreputable old caravan coming down the hillside. Look as if they had come out of the ark, or come at least from the North Pole, these crafty Gibeonites. Imagine the calm, serious faces with which they told this huge lie. What lie? "We are from a far country. We never hear of Ai, or Jericho, or Gibeon, or Jordan. Oh dear, no. Don't know where they are. How should we, in our far country?" Notice the cleverness of mentioning only the deeds in Egypt and beyond Jordan—the deeds long past. Why not mention crossing Jordan, or fall of Jericho or Ai? Repeat the lies about bread, clothes, wine-skins, etc. Yes, "We are poor innocent travellers, longing to be your friends. See how eager we are—how far we have come." So the Israelites believed them, ate bread with them—not the mouldy bread, we hope—made a league with them.

Do you wonder Israel was deceived? Would you have been? Was Israel to blame at all? Why? (*v.* 14). Why not trust their own common-sense? They must often have had to trust their common-sense; quite right in little things. God gave common-sense for that. But in important things? No. What should we do? Ever use our own sense and judgment? Is it wrong to trust them? Who gave them? But must not rely entirely on them. "O Lord, I know that the way of man is not in himself. It is not in man that walketh to direct his steps." Our own wishes often make us think an act looks right; we are easily biased. We should begin by submitting our lives altogether to God, and wishing to do what *He* would like—not merely what *we* would like. That state of mind is a great help to our judgment. But in every important thing what do? Ask counsel of the Lord. He will purify desires, calm your passions, divinely direct you. "Commit thy way unto the Lord."

§ 2. The Treaty Kept

How soon fraud discovered? Such a rage as Israelites were in! "Smite them—kill them. They have tricked us. They are Canaanites!" Did they kill them? Why not? Joshua and the princes saved them? Was it not good of them? Do you think they deserved to be killed? Perhaps so—perhaps not. At any rate a promise had been made, and those good princes thought that God would not like them to break a promise. Were they right? Yes, certainly. Is it ever right to break a promise?

Suppose you promised to steal or kill? Then it

would be a worse wrong to keep it—*e.g., Herod.* But should not have made it, and should ask God to forgive you for having made it. Be very careful about making promises. Great disgrace to religion to see a promise made and carelessly broken. *(Impress this on children: it is a frequent fault with them.)*

These leaders of Israel had to bear great unpopularity (*v.* 18). But they did what they thought right for God's sake. Sometimes even Christian men not so good. In 1444, at Battle of Varna, the Christian king, Ladislaus of Hungary, had made a league with the Mahometan sultan Amurath II. Even a clergyman, Cardinal Julian, persuaded him to break it. What a shame! The Polish clergy begged him to do right, but no use. The sultan (Mahometan) was so indignant he cried out to Jesus Christ to punish the Christian's treachery. What a disgrace to Christ and to religion! Joshua and his princes were better men. Long afterwards, in Saul's day, the treaty was broken, and God punished terribly for it (2 Samuel xxi. 1-9). How did Joshua punish Gibeonites? What might the Gibeonites have done instead of deceiving? Come honestly and candidly and told the truth. I am sure God's will would have been to receive them, and teach them to be good men.

Now, what do you think this chapter teaches us?

1st. What does it teach about deceiving?

2nd. About seeking guidance?

3rd. About promises?

Go into these as carefully as time permits. At the

close remind of baptismal promise, which has to be consciously renewed by each at Confirmation. Impress its seriousness, and the duty of earnest thought about it, before and after Confirmation.

QUESTIONS FOR LESSON V

Tell the clever trick of the Gibeonites.

Were Israelites deceived by it?

What did the Israelites promise these schemers?

By and by when they found out this trick Joshua and his men did rather a fine thing. What was it?

Did this please the Israelite crowd?

What do you think about it yourself?

Do you think it pleased God?

THE BATTLE OF BETH-HORON

Joshua X. to v. 15

(1) I think it is most unwise to hang any spiritual teaching on to this Lesson beyond what is plainly contained in it—the power of Joshua's prayer, and the fact that men are invincible if God be with them. It is dangerous work spiritualizing such chapters as this. If you make the Gibeonites a type of the good people who come out from evil companions to join the people of God, you will probably have quick-witted children who cannot help thinking it rather mean of the Gibeonites to play the traitor in order to save their own skins. They will probably not speak of it, but they will think it all the same; and it is most dangerous for children to associate God's favour with questionable deeds. Never let them do that. We do not know the merits of the case for the Gibeonites. The whole chapter, with its terrible carnage, is perhaps the most difficult in all the Bible to teach the children. It is capable of leaving evil impressions that may remain for life if it be not wisely taught. But let the teacher face it fearlessly, for he may do much good

with it. Let him try to give careful study to this standing difficulty of the Old Testament—the slaughter of the Canaanites. Read Lesson II and Introduction, Section 4. But if he still feels a difficulty about the subject, let him not try to "plead for God" against his conscience. The difficulty in our consciences arises from our ignorance of the whole facts of the case. Explain that to the children. Say, "If we knew the whole as God does, we should quite see that it was right." At the same time it will probably be best not to direct attention unnecessarily to the carnage in the chapter. There is another important difficulty, which it will be most useful to deal with.

(2) It is worth taking much trouble abut this chapter, if only for the sake of dealing with the difficulty of the "sun standing still," which has been so often a stumbling-block to earnest people. Explain it to this one generation, and we shall have gone far to remove one serious stumbling-block in the days to come. We can hardly over-estimate the widespread mischief that such misreadings of Holy Scripture are still doing and the power they give to the scoffer and unbeliever. Read carefully the explanation printed at the end of Lesson. It is a question whether it would not be best, for the elder classes at least, to leave out the spiritual teaching for this one day, and for this one most difficult chapter, and try to teach them thoroughly about this passage.

Remember last Lesson. Terror of kings and the Canaanite towns before the Israelites. Dread of the Almighty Power that had made Jordan divide and Jericho fall. All banded together to oppose Israel. One town dropped out—name? Remember their clever trick? Israel received them and promised to be their friend. Even when deceit discovered, Joshua would not cast them off. "No! we have promised to stand by them. We must keep our promise."

Very soon he had to do it. A few weeks afterwards messengers flying in hot haste down the pass to the Israelite camp. No old boots or old clothes this time. They reach the camp at Gilgal (see map); rush in breathless fright to the tent of the leader. "Oh, save us! save us! Come up quickly to help us! All the kings of the Amorites are gathered together against us! They are so angry because we have made friends with you!" (*v.* 6). "Have we plenty of time to save you?" "No—no. The kings and the armies are come already; they are encamped against Gibeon! The siege is begun (*v.* 5). We are lost unless you can come quickly!"

Now, this was a very dangerous expedition. To go up into the mountain passes, where five chiefs, with their armies, were encamped. Those Canaanites knew all the roads—all the hiding places—could easily prepare ambushes, and guard the passes and throw great rocks down upon the invaders. But Joshua was no laggard. He was a man prompt to decide. Did he take care to find out God's will this time? (*v.* 8). Not forget to inquire, as when Gibeonites first came. He found it was right to go. It was God's will. That was enough. Immediately the trumpets ring out through the host. The troops begin to gather in from every side. "We are off to the mountains to save Gibeon." "But it is nearly night already, and Gibeon is a long way off." "It matters not. Fall in quickly! Away! March!" And away into the night, up the dark mountain passes they go, with steady, rapid step. Not a moment was to be lost. Everything depended on surprising the enemy—getting in before he could suspect or be ready. Quickly, eagerly, excitedly the men press on through the darkness. Many hours have elapsed. The dawn is coming. They can see the dim outline of the hill of Gibeon, with its frowning cliffs, and the deep pass of Beth-Horon. There is the town now—there are the Canaanite armies around it. All is quiet. Nobody expects them. Picture to yourselves the excitement of the men.

A brief pause—then the ringing call of the trumpets, and the wild shout of Israel's battle-cry: "God is mighty in battle. God is His name!"[1] and in a moment the host is dashing upon the foe. The Canaanite soldiers spring to their arms. They close in fierce combat. But they cannot fight well. They are unprepared, utterly surprised—no time to fall into order. Terror is upon them of this mysterious, conquering Israel—terror of Jehovah. And even as they fight they hear the thunder rolling, and the sky is growing black, and the big hail-stones are already bounding off their shields. Surely, Jehovah, the God of Israel, is against them! Away they fly, in superstitious terror, up the sloping hillside— through the frowning cliffs of the Pass of Beth-Horon, with the great hailstones, bigger and bigger, crashing upon their heads.

Joshua is after them in hot pursuit. He sees now the enormous importance of this battle. Like Waterloo, on which peace of Europe depended. Chief power of

[1] So the Samaritan Book of Joshua gives the battle-cry.

Canaan is flying before him. If he can utterly defeat them, the whole conquest of Palestine is secure. Instead of many years of fighting and struggling, to-day can end it all, if only he has entire success. Oh! that he could get time before night to finish the victory!

He is standing at the summit of the pass; the enemy are rushing down in wild confusion; if the night comes on, they will escape in the darkness, and the fruits of his great victory will be lost. What can he do? He can do nothing. But he knows that God can. And with eager longing he lifts his heart to God, and utters his impassioned cry, as he sees the sunbeams resting upon Gibeon: "O sun, rest thou still upon Gibeon; and thou, moon, in the valley of Ajalon!" Let the day be lengthened—let the night be delayed—until we have completed this victory for Israel!

Did God hear him? Yes. An unusually bright evening, clear daylight extending longer than usual, and Israel completed that day the greatest victory of its warfare. The possession of all Palestine was secured by the result of this one conflict. "All these kings and their lands did Joshua take at *one* time, because the Lord fought for Israel." It was the greatest day, the greatest victory, in the whole history of Israel. Indeed, it was one of the great decisive battles of the world. Greater than Marathon, or Hastings, or Waterloo, or defeat of Armada; for, humanly speaking, it decided the fortunes of Israel and the Canaanites. The extinction of Israel would have meant the blotting out of the light of God in the world. By means of this victory Israel was now free to settle down to the great work for the sake of all mankind—the work of training a godly people, and writing and teaching the Bible, and preparing for the coming of the Messiah into the world.

Now, what do you think is the lesson we learn? (Let the children guess freely. Teach them to use their minds about it; then lead them to the thought—"If God be with us, who can be against us?") With all the difficulties of the story, we know at any rate that Israel was fighting on the side of God and righteousness. Illustrate by unpopularity at school, because refuse to join in something that God would not approve of. Never mind. God is with you. Be faithful to God, and He will conquer for you, as for Israel. Who gave the Israelites victory? Joshua? No. It was God. He heard Joshua's prayer. "The Lord harkened to the voice of a man." He did what Joshua wanted about the lengthening of the day. How? We don't know. Do you think the sun really stood still? Does the sun really move at all round the earth? No; it stands still always, and the earth goes round it. Do you think the earth stopped turning round on its axis? We have no reason at all to think so. Could God have stopped the sun and the earth and all the planets in a moment? Yes, certainly. But there is no reason to think any such improbable thing was done. (See Explanation. For children a few words will suffice. For older pupils teach fully, as in following note on the passage. But, with all, take care to emphasize the misreading.)

NOTE ON "THE SUN STANDING STILL"

Joshua x.

Before attempting any explanation, let it be clearly understood that there is no question as to *what God could have done.* Many objections have been urged, such as the impossibility of stopping the motions of the heavenly bodies—the disturbance that would be caused throughout the solar system, etc. We need have no hesitation in saying that the God who made the solar system, and set it going, could easily have performed greater miracles than the providing for this. But while we cannot think anything impossible with God, we may quite fairly think certain things *improbable.* We are bound, in such a case at any rate, to ask, "Does the Bible even assert that it was done?" And the answer of any careful scholar will be, "No, it does not." We can but very briefly explain here.

First, notice that the statement is a quotation from the old lost Book of Jasher—probably the book of the war-songs of Israel (see *v.* 13; 2 Samuel i. 18, R.V.). Now here, in the midst of the prose history, we have this poetical quotation in metrical form, surely a strong presumption that it was intended but as a poetic figure to express the lengthening of the clear daylight for Israel. It is worth notice in this connection that the other edition of the Book of Joshua—the Samaritan edition—leaves out this piece of poetry, and tells the story in prose only. It says no word of the sun or moon standing still, but simply this—"The day was lengthened at Joshua's prayer." It never thinks of such a misreading of the passage. Neither does Josephus, the Jewish historian. "The day was increased," he says, "lest night should check their zeal." (*Antiquities of the Jews*, v 1, §17). And evidently the inspired prophets and psalmists had no thought of such a prosaic meaning to a poetical figure. They are continually celebrating God's wonders in those days of Moses and Joshua— the manna, the plagues, the crossing the sea, etc.; but of this, which, if it had happened, would have been the most stupendous miracle since the world began, they say absolutely nothing. It seems to have made no impression at all on them. Why? Surely because they were Easterners, and accustomed to poetic description, and therefore understood what the writer meant. Fancy any sensible man reading literally these lines:—

"And far away the red sun kissed the sea."

Or these lines from Bishop Hannington's last journal, describing a long and weary day:—"How often I gazed at the sun; it stood still in the heavens, and would not go down." Or the many similar passages in the Bible, *e.g.:* —

"The stars in their courses fought against Sisera."
"The mountains skipped like rams."
"The morning stars sang together."

Or that beautiful piece of imagery in Habakkuk iii. 10, 11:—

"The mountains saw Thee and trembled;
The deep lifted up his hands on high;
The sun and the moon stood still in their habitation,
At the shining of Thy glittering spear."

Many people think that this is a reference to the miracle in Joshua. If so, it only makes the argument stronger; for if all the rest of the passage about the mountains and the deep be clearly figurative, why should this one line be read otherwise?

What the Scripture asserts, then, is, that in some way God gave lengthened-out daylight, in answer to Joshua's impassioned prayer. On account of this, Israel gained the greatest victory in its annals, utterly demolished a powerful league of civilized kings, and practically won Palestine. No wonder that the poet, in the Book of Jasher, should so vividly tell of the fact that the sun remained in the heavens till the great victory was complete. The only wonder seems to be that this passage, above all other similar passages in Scripture, should ever have been so misread, and that this misreading should have been so obstinately held to in our own day. Probably the explanation is to be partly found in the prominence given to the passage in Galileo's days. When he asserted that the received system of astronomy was wrong, and that the sun does not really move round the earth at all, he was denounced as contradicting the Word of God; and this text in Joshua, ignorantly misinterpreted, became the centre of the great battle between the astronomers and the theologians. "God says in Joshua that the sun does go round the earth." It was felt to be unsound and irreligious to give up this point; and the effects of this feeling have remained in some degree since; and the result has been very mischievous in our days, when it is clearly seen that Galileo was right, and the theologians were wrong. It is worth while taking trouble to correct the mistake, if only to save the pupils in their after-days from the force of the infidel sneers on the subject. Space here forbids a fuller and more adequate treatment of the passage.

QUESTIONS FOR LESSON VI

Now the crafty Gibeonites got caught for their trick. By whom?

What did Joshua decide to do?

Did the tricksters deserve that he should save them?

Why did he do it?

Why was victory here so important?

What did Joshua pray as the darkness came?

Do you think the sun really stood still or that the earth stopped revolving?

Could God have done that?

Why do we think He did not?

Yet He answered Joshua's prayer. How?

CALEB—SOLDIERS OF GOD

Joshua XIV., XV. vv. 16-20, XIX. 49 to end

Recapitulate briefly last Lesson. Remind of the great results of Battle of Beth-Horon—practically put an end to the war, and gave possession of Palestine, so that Joshua could now proceed to the dividing of the land.

Remember Battle of Hastings in England? Who won? Who were defeated? Result was that England was completely in the Norman's power. William the Conqueror sat with his chiefs, and divided up England. Great clamouring of chiefs for the best places—strifes and jealousies. King gave best lands to his special favourites or to the powerful chiefs whom he most feared or most wanted. Greedy, selfish, godless way of dividing.

§ 1. Soldiers of God

See Joshua in the Great Tent dividing the land. Who with him arranging the distribution? (*v.* 1). Yes, head of the Church and head of the State, and the heads of the

65

tribes, all to see fair play. How divided? Like Normans? Grasping, striving, fighting for best place? No (*v.* 2). By lot, as the Lord commanded. Perhaps a number of names thrown into bag, and each drew out one. Remember other decision by lot? (Achan, Lesson IV). In New Testament (Acts i. 26). Seems like chance, but when God directed it, you may be sure it would be a right division. No man's ambition, or greediness, or scheming had any place. The whole matter was reverently, unselfishly referred to God. They had a belief that God would guide in such a case (Proverbs xvi. 33). Do you think He would? Yes, and we never hear of any strife afterwards about this division. Each took what was allotted. All was fair.

One day they hear outside the tramp of warriors, the shouting of people. What is it? It is the men of Judah bringing in their hero, old Caleb, the son of Jephunneh, to be appointed his inheritance. It was said he was no Israelite by birth, but one perhaps of the mixed multitude that followed Israel out of Egypt (Exodus xii. 38), who, for his valour and virtues, received a part among the children of Judah (Joshua xv. 13). But he was evidently a great favourite with his tribe; and I think the writer of this history writes about him as if he loved him too. See him meeting with his old comrade, now the chief of Israel. Hear him remind him of "what the Lord said to Moses concerning thee and me in Kadesh-barnea." Do you remember it? What happened there? Read Numbers xiv. 30. Now do you remember? Forty-five years before, when these two were young warriors of Israel, Moses sent them out as two of the twelve spies.

The people were faithless and cowardly, and so were the spies, all except these two. Remember their report? Read Numbers xii. 32, 33; xiii. 1. Keep Bibles open at this place. The poor cowardly set who forgot the power of their God, and only thought of the great giants, and the big cities, and the terror of being "eaten up" by that unknown land (Numbers xiii. 32). But there were two brave men who had courage and faith in God. They saw with disgust the howling mob crying and rebelling against God in their terror, and they threw their whole powers into the effort to arouse them. "Oh! don't be cowards: it is a good land, and the Lord is with us: fear them not!" It was a daring thing for two men to throw themselves thus in opposition to a raging mob. And they very nearly paid with their lives for it. What happened? (Numbers viii. 10). Don't you admire that daring spirit? They were but two against a multitude, and they dared everything for sake of God and the right. They were but two. Do you remember a similar case of three? Is there a grander scene in the history of the world than the three heroes in Babylon with the angry king before them and the raging fire behind them? "If it be so, our God whom we serve is able to deliver us; *but if not,* even if He see not fit to deliver us, yet we will not serve thy gods, nor worship the golden image which thou hast set up." You, who have courage perhaps to *fight,* have you courage to bear for sake of God and the right? When your school-fellows and comrades laugh at you, and call names because you are resolved to be true to the vows of your baptism, try to think of God and His delight in courage. Try to think of Joshua and Caleb, so unpopular in such danger. Try to think of the three young rulers who stood alone for God before the power of Babylon. If you find wrong-doing, and refuse to join; if you find a young comrade going wrong, and take courage to speak to him—it is not easy—it may make you unpopular; but is it not a glorious thing to bear it for Christ? There is no courage in shipwreck or battlefield greater or dearer to God than the courage which resolves, "I will be true to God at any cost of pain, or loss, or unpopularity!" Listen to Caleb telling without pride or arrogance (you can see how humble and religious he is), "I have wholly followed the Lord my God!" Men like that are always loved and respected at last. Look at these two old men, the only survivors of the old Egyptian slaves. All the rest dead in the wilderness. There they stand, one the chief of Israel, one a plain, poor soldier still; but both loved and honoured by the people around them, and resting gladly in the favour of God. All their lives they have been God's true soldiers. His soldiers and servants they will be to their lives' end.

§ 2. *The Giant-Killer*

What promise of Moses does Caleb plead? (*v.* 9). The place where Caleb had spied out should be his. Was he to get it without fighting? Was it an easy place that he asked for? No; the big cities were there still, and the old giants, the children of Anak, were ready to crush him. How old was Caleb now? Is it not like the story of Jack the Giant-Killer? This little soldier, with his grey hairs, and his eighty-five years of age, going off to the mountains to attack the giants!

For they were real giants, those sons of Anak, like Goliath of Gath. Hebron was the City of the Four Giants—Anak, Aheman, Sheshai, Talmai (Numbers xiii. 22). Can't you fancy him, like Jack the Giant-Killer, sounding his trumpet, and the huge, lumbering giants coming out to attack him! Was it a foolish daring to attack such a place? No; it was the same old daring of his youth—the daring that comes from trust in God (Joshua xiv. 12)—"If the Lord be with me." That was the secret of Caleb's courage. So his old comrade blessed him, and gave him the land to conquer. Does God give you inheritance, too? But you must fight your way to it. You have giants, too, to fight in the path to your inheritance. You may have still worse giants in the days to come, if you are really going to fight for God. Tell me of some of your giants? (1) *Evil in your heart.* —Bad habits, laziness, fear, worldliness, etc. *Temptations outside.* —Examples of others, customs of your society, etc. (2) *Opposition.* —Unpopularity, loss, misunderstanding. What is your hope of victory? Same as Caleb's: "If the Lord will be with me, I shall be able to drive them out." Illustrate. Boy who has learned this soldier spirit of religion. Feels strong temptation to ill-temper. Just about to hit out when he remembers that to conquer this will be one of his victories for God. Goes off instantly to fight it out alone, and in a moment the battle with Satan is over. The ill-temper is gone. "The Lord is with me; I am able to drive it out."

QUESTIONS FOR LESSON VII

What were Joshua and the Chiefs now engaged in?

Who was Caleb and what is he here for?

What sort of man is he?

He reminds Joshua of a great enterprise in which they both had joined in Moses' day. What was it?

Why did we think of him as "the Giant-Killer"?

Repeat the words which show the secret of his courage, "If the Lord be with me," etc.

LESSON VIII

THE PLACE OF REFUGE

Joshua XX., XXI. v. 41 to end

The main thought in this Lesson should be the Refuge in Christ, which, unlike the Cities of Refuge, is available for the *guilty*. If there is not sufficient time for the whole, Section 2, on the Progressive Teaching of Scripture, may be very briefly dealt with. But it is a most important subject for senior classes, and may save them from much doubt and difficulty about Old Testament teaching in after years.

§ 1. Need of Refuge Cities

Read chapter xx. What is it about? Cities of refuge for *murderers?* No. What sort of killing? Did you ever hurt some one by accident? Does killing by accident deserve punishment as killing intentionally does? But with half-savage nations like the Jews they did not stop to think about that. If a man killed your brother in those days, the custom was that you should pursue and kill him. If not, you would be disgraced as a coward. Then, if you succeeded in killing the slayer, his friends would pursue and kill you; and so it would go on for many years. This custom long ago in the days of Joshua was necessary to prevent intentional murders—no properly executed laws to prevent them—but often led to terrible wrong, and cruelty, and revenge.

Now look at *v.* 1. Is this first mention? No. Long ago directed by God when they should be in possession of the land. Now, therefore, they were to do it. (Teacher should read Exodus xxi. 13, and selected parts of sections beginning Numbers xxxv. 9; Deuteronomy xix. 2; especially Numbers xxxv. 20-25, showing that the right of asylum did not protect a murderer.) How many cities? Where? Three each side Jordan. Why? Name some of them. Old Caleb's city was one of them (*v.* 6). (See last Lesson.) So Caleb must have beaten his big giants. Were they cities of escape or cities of judgment? Were they for the innocent or the guilty? Yes; really refuge, where a man was kept safe from mob till he could be tried. Who judged him? (Numbers xxxv. 24). If innocent, what? If guilty? They gave him up to the avenger of blood (*v.* 21). The Christian Church in middle ages gave right of asylum in churches. If a man fled there, he was safe. But it was abused. Guilty could escape as well as innocent. So this law of Moses about Cities of Refuge was a very good one.

§ 2. Progressive Teaching

Why did not God make a law, as He has for Christians in later days, that they should love their enemies, and give up all thought of revenge? Would not that be easier than building cities? Besides, the cities did not always save a man. If the avenger caught him on the road, he would kill him. Why not give the higher Christian law? Because not yet ready for higher teaching. A half-savage race was not yet fit for it. God had to teach the world slowly—gradually. The fuller, higher teaching only came with Jesus Christ.

In olden days it was enough to say, "Love your *neighbour.*" Our Lord added higher teaching: "Love your *enemies*, too." Thus a missionary to the poor negroes in Africa, who think very little of murder, and robbery, and wickedness of every kind, has to begin at first with the lower and easier commands. He knows that the impure, dishonest, bloody savage is not yet ready for the fullness of Christian life—that self-sacrifice and love of enemies and full consecration of himself to God are too much to expect at present. So he tells him only: "Don't worship idols. Don't kill. Do not steal," etc. By-and-by he goes on to higher teaching about loving his enemies, and such-like. That was God's way of teaching mankind. That is the reason you find higher teaching in New Testament than in the Old. Do you remember how our Lord tells us that: "Think not that I came to destroy the law or the prophets. I am not come to destroy, but to *fill up*" (that which is deficient)? Let the teacher study carefully St. Matthew v. 17, 21-2, 33-34, 38-39, 43-44. It will be well worth while teaching even a little of this lesson of *God's progressive teaching of humanity*. It may save many a pupil from doubts and difficulties about the Old Testament teaching, in after days.

§ 3. The Avenger of Blood

Now picture the poor fugitive, gasping and blood-stained, with clothes torn and muddy, running for his life. He had been perhaps shooting at game in the wood, and the arrow had glanced aside and pierced a man's heart; or chopping wood, and the axe-head had slipped off and killed a man. He had not meant to kill him, but he knows that will not save him. Instantly he thinks of the nearest Refuge City—thankful for its existence. Before evening the dead man's family will know, and the avenger of blood will be on the track. He flings down his bow and arrows, and away, away for dear life he starts, tearing through the thickets, plunging through the rivers, avoiding every public place.

Poor fellow! he may be a good and noble-minded man; but he must die if the avenger catches him. Now he hears the horns sounding through the mountains, and the wailing and shouting of the dead man's friends. They are rousing the whole country-side for the chase, and with double speed the fugitive flies on. All night long he struggles through the darkness. At dawn he can see right up the hill Kirjath Arba, the city of Caleb. Can he reach it? The pursuers are scattered on all sides; most of them have dropped out, as in a long paper-chase when the hounds grow tired. But in the front there are swift runners, and foremost of all is the son of the dead man, with stern set face and untiring limbs. Nearer and nearer they get to the town; closer and closer the pursuers creep on; the fugitive is but fifty yards from the gates; the pursuer's spear flies past his head; one mad spurt, and he throws himself panting, and gasping, and

74

half-dead upon the ground, but inside the gate!—saved! "O thanks be to God!" he would cry, "for this city of refuge to save a helpless, innocent man."

§ 4. *Our Refuge*

Now let us think of the teaching for ourselves. When men commit sin now, there is an avenger behind them, too, tracking their steps. Even if a man should escape punishment of the law, yet he does not escape the avenger—he bears the punishment and curse within. He has also the dread of a worse punishment hereafter. Is there any refuge? Could you direct him? Yes, flee to the Lord Jesus Christ. He has found the Refuge. He who has been the One injured and pained by our sin—who might with some justice have been the avenger, He founds the City of Refuge for us all.

> "All the souls that were forfeit once,
>   And He that might the vantage best have took
>   Found out the remedy."

How is His Refuge, different from those of Joshua? (1) Who only were saved in those? Innocent. What of guilty? No use for the guilty to flee to those. What of the guilty who flee to Christ? What a sad thing for wretched, guilty sinner if he were told no hope unless innocent! How can the guilty be saved by our Lord? Suppose he remains wicked, can he gain the refuge? Christ's refuge is refuge from sin as well as punishment. Must really repent and turn to Him. (2) Men fled to the cities for *justice*. They flee to Christ for *mercy*. (3) And there is one difference more that you should specially learn. The fugitive in Joshua's day must give up his work, and happiness, and home, and friends, and be a poor exile in the far-off city in order to escape. In coming to Christ does he need to do that? No! he need give up no pleasure except it be a sinful one. The happy boy or girl gets more happiness in life; the fretted men and women get bright, restful, peaceful lives. It is the happiest thing on earth to be a servant of Christ. There is no other way of a really happy life here and hereafter but the coming into the blessed refuge under the shadow of His wings.

QUESTIONS FOR LESSON VIII

What were the Cities of Refuge for?

Why were they needed?

Would they save a wilful murderer?

Picture in words the fugitive and the avenger of blood after him.

Were the refuge cities a good plan?

But would it not be still better to teach the avengers and everybody to love their enemies?

Why would not this work out in those days?

Do you know what is meant by "God's *gradual* education of humanity"?

LESSON IX

THE STORY OF A MISUNDERSTANDING

Joshua XXII.

§ 1. The Comrades' Farewell

The allotting of the lands is over at last; Joshua and Phinehas and the heads of the tribes have finished their task. What comes next in our story? Ever seen a review? or any big gathering of soldiers? Have to tell of one to-day. Great plain of Shiloh amid the mountains: covered with tents and gay with banners, brilliant dresses, and the quick flashing of spears and armour in the sun. The trumpets are ringing out for marshalling troops. Men and women and little children are gathering in on every side from the woods and the mountains—from the far-off villages. Now, the steady tramp, tramp of an approaching band of soldiers. See the crowd open out for them at the end. In long line, rapidly, steadily, they come. Three great regiments—the soldiers of Reuben—the soldiers of Gad—the half-band of Manassites. On they go, followed by the cheers and the weeping of the crowd. For they are the brave comrades from beyond the Jordan, who have so faithfully and unselfishly stood by them in all their dangers. And now they have come together to say good-bye, and go home. (Remind the class of beginning of Book of Joshua, how these tribes had already got their inheritance beyond Jordan, and had nobly and generously, at Joshua's request, crossed the river, and dared all dangers of war, and lost many brave warriors, in order to help their brethren. Read Joshua i. 12-16). And now they are to go home, and the old chief has called them together to thank them and bless them, and bid them farewell. Tell me his words of thanks? Or dismissal? Of advice? (*vv.* 1-6). Was it not good advice? Like a father would give to his boy going away from home. Does it not show how deep and real Joshua's religion was? Sometimes people advise you when going out into the world: Be wise—be saving—make money—get rich—try to be prosperous. Are these good things to advise? Yes. But they are only the least important. What will give us truest happiness—money—or noble lives? Could we have high, pure happiness without much riches? Yes. Could we have it without living true, faithful lives for God? No. Did Joshua wish them to be rich and prosperous? Yes (*v.* 8). But the chief thing, in his view, was that they should have the blessing of a life lived for God. Tell me again his advice? (*v.* 5).

The trumpets ring out again, the three regiments fall into ranks. Right wheel! March! And with tears in their eyes, as they hear the old leader's blessing, as they listen to the cheering of the old comrades, and the sobbing of the women and children, the heroes march out and away through the mountains to the Jordan banks—to their own homes. What a pleasant parting, with the blessing and praise of their leader, and the loving farewells of their comrades. And yet within a few weeks those comrades were about to fly at their throats, and all on account of a stupid misunderstanding.

§ 2. The Misunderstanding

Some weeks have passed since the Israelites had sent away the three regiments, when strange, vexatious tidings came to them across the Jordan. What? (*v.* 11). What harm was it? Broke the commandments of God (Deuteronomy xii. 4-14; Leviticus xvii. 4). There was one central place appointed for sacrifice. They could pray to God in their own homes, and learn about Him. But only in one place must they offer sacrifice. Where? Shiloh.

Two reasons for this—(1st) Heathen altars were all over the land. If they could sacrifice on any altar, they must use the heathen altars, and soon get corrupted into filthy heathen worship; (2nd) It was necessary to keep the Church of Israel always one—not let it split up into separate little bodies. Must not do what is right in own eyes. "Not offer thine offerings in every place thou seest." (Deuteronomy xii. 8, 13). You see to-day how Christianity is weakened and God's work injured because Christians do not show one united front—one central worship—one body worshipping together the one God. Before this, Korah, Dathan, and Abiram tried to set up a separate worship. Was God pleased? What happened? Long afterwards Jeroboam did it (1 Kings xii. 27, etc.), and both the evils came that this law guarded against—separation and idolatry. Does that law exist still? Yes. God's law of unity has never been changed. Our Lord wanted the same unity kept. He prayed for His Church (John xvii. 21), *that they all may be one, in order that* the world, looking on this united band, should see that it was of Divine origin. Do Christians obey that law, and carry out that prayer of Christ? No. That is one of the sins of Christianity. See separate bodies of Christians all baptized into Christ's name, and will not worship together. Is it right? No. We should all worship together, and be one united body. What a grand work the Church could do here if all the people were united into one Church. Never mind whose the fault. We want to put away the evil from amongst us. It is a great evil. More than 200 different sects existing to-day. In Foreign Missions it puzzles the poor heathen. Told to join the Church of Christ, and they ask: Where is it? Which is it? In Madras nine different religious bodies within sight of each other. In China about thirty different sects. Must be sad for our Lord to see. Yet these divided Christians all love their God. If they could be brought to see the evil, they would perhaps put an end to it. Let us sympathize and help in efforts for Reunion, and pray that all divided Christians may learn to love and understand each other better and see this evil clearly, that thus it may be put away.

§ 3. The Explanation

What was result when Israelites heard the report? Angry words, fierce accusations, and in a few days the tribes were up in arms and on the brink of a fierce civil war. Happily there were some who, in their kindly remembrance of the old, generous fellow-soldiers, tried to think the best of them. There are always some of these reasonable, kindly-souled people who are not too eager to believe evil of their neighbours; they help to keep the world sweet, and kindly, and charitable. They said, "Perhaps they have not done it; only fair to ask them first at any rate." So they sent—whom? (*vv.* 13, 14). And off they went through the mountain passes to the Jordan. Alas, as they drew near to the bank of the river, there was the great altar plain before their eyes! Now surely the fault was beyond question. And very angrily Phinehas and the princes spake (*vv.* 16-20).

Yet all the time the men were absolutely innocent. Look how surprised and hurt they are; how eagerly they explain (*vv.* 22-29). "Rebel against God!" Set up a rival altar! Why, it was for the very opposite reason we did it—to keep up the memory of God—to keep up the unity of Israel! Oh, we never meant to do wrong. We did build the altar; but not a real altar for sacrifices, only a pattern, a memorial (*v.* 28), to remind our children of the altar of God in Shiloh. They were really brave, good, righteous men, was it not hard on them to be so suspected? They were so anxious about the religion of their children, and so anxious to keep close to God themselves, that they made this memorial altar. And

81

now look at the evil meaning that suspicious men had put on it.

So at last it dawned on these hasty Israelites that they had been judging their friends wrongly, and had very nearly brought on a terrible war. Were they glad or vexed to find mistake? (*v.* 30). Yes. They were good men, eager for religion, though hasty and suspicious; so they were glad, and they and all the tribes thanked God that their brethren had not sinned, and that they themselves had been saved from doing a cruel wrong.

§ 4. Lessons

In the history of the Church there have always been zealous, hasty people, quick to misunderstand, quick to see heresy and wrong where it was not perhaps meant. So too in lives of individual people. In ordinary life always some people quick to misunderstand, to see wrong and slights put on them where people never meant—to put bad meanings upon innocent actions. Nearly all the quarrels and separations between good people come of misunderstanding each other. Therefore learn—

(a) Not to be quick at suspecting evil of others. Charity "thinketh no evil." There is some good in everybody, a great deal of good in some. Let us get sharp-eyed to see the good, not sharp-eyed to see the evil. You know how hard it is when you are misjudged yourself. Try to think the best of others, and to put the best construction on their acts that you can.

(b) Always prevent misunderstanding with your friend by speaking straight to him about it. Never condemn unheard. It may look very bad against him. So it did against Reubenites when the altar was seen; yet they were innocent. Oh! Many a friendship has been broken for ever through not having courage to "have it out" candidly and kindly with your friend alone. Remember our Lord's advice: "Tell him his fault between thee and him alone." There is a beautiful text in the Apocryphal Book of Wisdom:—

"Admonish a friend: it may be he hath not done it, or if he hath done it, that he do it no more.

"Admonish a friend: it may be he hath not said it, or if he hath said it, that he say it no more.

"Admonish a friend: it may be but a slander; do not believe every tale."

(c) Always remember when misjudged and misunderstood by your friend that you have One Friend who never misjudges—never misunderstands—who knows your every thought, who is not wanting to pick holes in you or find fault with you, but, like your own mother, always looking for the good and hoping to see it. He can see the good motive at the bottom of the mistaken action. He can see the sorrow and penitence in your heart when people around see only your failure and sin. (If time to do so, illustrate by His treatment of the three who fell asleep at Gethsemane: "The spirit is willing; it is only the flesh is weak;" by His kind message after Peter's denial: "Go tell My disciples *and Peter*;" and other instances of like kind.) Therefore never be afraid to come to Him with your faults.

"His love beyond a brother's.
Oh! how He loves!"

QUESTIONS FOR LESSON IX

Who were the three great regiments marching eastward?

What fine thing had they done for their comrades?

Now in a few months a bad story about them comes back to these comrades. What was it?

Was it true?

It nearly led to slaughter. How?

What was the simple explanation of it?

What should it teach us about (1) lightly suspecting evil, (2) speaking straight to the suspected friend?

What pleasant thing does it remind us of about Our Lord?

LESSON X

AN OLD MAN'S ADVICE

Joshua XXIV.

Last chapter now of our hero's life-story. Slave-boy had become a chieftain. God's chieftain. Had fought God's battles. Divided God's promised land. And then, when too old for active work, retired to rest at—where? There twenty years of happy, holy, restful life—reverenced by the people, blessed by God—exercising a powerful influence on the side of righteousness (see Judges ii. 7). "A good old age" is how the Bible describes such lives.

Then one day a hurried message came from Timnath Serah—to every corner of the land. No post. No telegraphs. Do any of you remember Roderick Dhu and the Fiery Cross, in *The Lady of the Lake?* To every village, and town, and mountain dwelling came the call—"The chief wants to see his old fellow-solders and all the leaders and officers of Israel." What interest it would arouse. Think of the day of Napoleon's escape from Elba, and the old comrades' excitement at the thought of meeting their general again. Still more delightful here. Not only a great general, whom they almost adored, but also what Napoleon was not—a high-souled, heroic, unselfish, godly man. Only of God, and of duty, and of the welfare of the people.

Try to call up the scene. The crowds of old warriors and chiefs of the people. The wild enthusiasm as the white-haired chieftain came forth. The memories of the old battle-days—of Jordan and Jericho, and the fierce fight of Beth-Horon. How their hearts would be stirred. How they would listen and treasure his words. He is glad to see them again; but has he sent for them only for that? No, what else? He has something to say to them—something very serious. He feels life ebbing away. He is going, he says, the way of all the earth (xxiii. 14), to his eternal rest; and, like a good old father at the close of life, he is anxious about these children committed to him by God fifty years ago. What does he talk about?

§ 1. He Talks about the Past Days

Old men often *do* talk about themselves, and boast of what they have done. Did Joshua? No. Little thought of self. All of God, who had been so good to them (*vv.* 3-6). Class keep looking at Bible: tell me briefly what he reminded them of? (*vv.* 1-13). Yes, the goodness of God in the days of the patriarchs, in the slavery of Egypt, through the dangerous times when Moses led, through his own half-century of rule—whole subject, the goodness of God, the undeserved blessings. Marvelous victories, not by *their* strength or *their* arms. Most old men who have lived for God have same experience. (An old man of very afflicted life told writer, "Every day I am more inclined to cry, 'Surely goodness and mercy have followed me,' etc." Tell any such cases.) We often see but little to thank God for. Don't think enough. Try to make realize. Put your hands on your heart. Feel your hearts beating, lungs rising and falling. What happens if stopped? What makes them go on? Could doctor tell? No. They go on just the same in your sleep. Every instant danger of death if stopped. Who is moving them? Think of ears, eyes, brain engaged now. Of the corn and fruit ripening outside. Of homes, parents, friends, games, pleasures, prospects. Has not God been good to you? Have not goodness and mercy followed you all the days of your life?

§ 2. He Talks about the Days to Come

Why has he begun by talking of the past? What conclusion does he draw? Because God so good. Now, *therefore*. Meaning of *therefore*. For that reason (*v.* 14), fear the Lord, and serve Him in sincerity and truth. Turn from idolatry and all sin. God is so good to you. Do not give pain to Him in return. Joshua knows all their weakness and the temptations around them. He knew some did not care much. He wants to rouse them. So he offers them a choice. What choice? He appeals. If not serve God, whom serve? (*v.* 15). "Choose," he says, "between God and idols." He is mocking. He means, You know there is no question which is worth serving.

Look to your future; think of the choice. On one hand, Evil; on other, Good; on one hand, folly, sinfulness, a godless, selfish life, and a hopeless, helpless death. On the other hand, to lead pure, noble, helpful days; to make life bright and happy for others; to be "Christ's faithful soldiers and servants to your lives' end," and after your lives' end to be with God for ever. Now, here are the two sides—which is the better? It would be only mocking, like Joshua, if I said, Choose. Do you believe that there is any question as to which is the better? Do you believe that the utterly best thing in the whole world is to be good, even if never to be rewarded for it? That the utterly worst thing in the whole world is to be bad, even if never to be punished for it? And then there are the eternal consequences, too. Do men ever deliberately *choose* bad life? Very seldom, I think. But they drift into it without choosing. Take care.

§ 3. He Tells His Own Choice

An old man's choice; had tried a lifetime of God's service. He ought to know. What is his advice to others? "Serve ye the Lord in sincerity and truth." (*v.* 14). What his resolve for himself? (*v.* 15). "As for me and my house we will serve the Lord." Yes. He has chosen God, and right and duty, when young. Now in old age, he is glad of it, and certain that he was right. No regrets for the early choice. No doubts about its wisdom. The longer any man's experience in that service the more satisfaction with it. Do you think anybody ever heard an old Christian say, "I'm sorry I chose God"? Or that anybody ever heard an old worldling say, "I'm glad I did not choose God"? No. God's old men are all happy. The devil has no happy old men.

"As for me and my house," etc.: what effect on the people? (*v.* 16). Yes. And the people were deeply moved as they heard the voice that had often cheered them to battle and guided them in counsel now pleading with them to be faithful to God. They knew no blesseder lot could be theirs than to follow the steps of that kingly old man. And as from one heart the eager shout went up: "We too, will serve the Lord. God forbid that we should forsake the Lord." (*v.* 16). God help you to make that resolve too. Is it not a touching scene? Is it not a fit ending to that hero-life? We have seen him as a slave-boy, as a soldier, as a ruler, always loyal and faithful to God. We look our last on him now as he stands pleading with his people, and that people, moved by a mighty impulse for good, are promising in the presence of God to be His servants for ever.

QUESTIONS FOR LESSON X

Picture in words the meeting of the aged Joshua and his people.

What does he tell them about the old days past?

What does he advise about the future?

Tell me the words of his own life choice, "As for me," etc.

Do you think any aged Christian ever said, "I am sorry I chose God"?

"The Devil has no happy old people." Explain.

PART II

THE STORY OF
THE JUDGES

Lecture to the Teacher

Let me earnestly advise the teacher, before beginning the teaching of this Book, to spend at least a week of his spare time in reading and re-reading it again and again, and, if possible, with the help of such books as Stanley's *Jewish Church,* until he has acquired a thorough grasp of its history, and entered, at least in some degree, into its spirit. It will well repay the trouble spent on it. It is not the most important or the most edifying, but it will be the teacher's fault if it is not the most fascinating part of the whole Jewish history. There is absolutely no excuse for a dull lesson in teaching this Book of Judges.

I

First of all, the heroes are so intensely human, and so much at our own level, that we cannot help being in sympathy with them. Moses and Joshua we had to admire from afar; they seemed immeasurably above us in the nobleness of their characters. But here we have a set of rough, impulsive, passionate men, not half civilized, not half sanctified, and yet used by God as the champions and saviours of His people. Perhaps it is that we are encouraged for ourselves by the fact of God's using such men—perhaps it is that we can the better understand them on account of their very faults and defects—perhaps it is that some of us have an innate liking for impulsiveness and adventure such as puts us in touch with the freaks of a wild, good-natured, mischievous schoolboy, even in things for which we blame him.

Whatever the cause, there is a freshness and interest about these heroes of the Book of Judges that is bound to lay hold on us, if we only take the trouble of understanding them, and entering into their circumstances. And, besides this interest, arising from sympathy with the heroes, there is a deep source of interest in the story itself. It is as full of stirring romance as any story of chivalry in the middle ages. Stories of sore oppression—of brutal tyranny—of heroes rising to right the wrong—of stern patriot-soldiers dashing themselves against forces ten times their number, eager to sweep the oppressor from the earth. Think of a boy's delight in deeds of heroism and adventure; in the stories of Marryat, and Ballantyne, and Henty. Why, none of them have such magnificent opportunities as you have in this story of gratifying it to the full. Think of Gideon's night march, and the stratagem of the pitchers—think of the tragic pathos of Jephthah's meeting with his daughter—think of Deborah, like another Joan of Arc, rousing her people to wild enthusiasm for liberty—think of the big, mischievous giant with the gates of Gaza on his back, laughing to himself at the surprise of the thick-headed Philistines whom he had outwitted.

No part of the Bible gives such scope for vivid word-pictures. The book is crammed full of them. There is no history in the world more full of colour, and romance, and stirring incident than this piece of old-world lore which you are teaching. Let no teacher say, "I have not the power of picturing." It is mainly a question of taking trouble about it. No doubt, some have keener sympathies and quicker imaginative powers than others; but there is no one who will take the trouble of entering into this history, and trying to put himself in the place of its heroes and its sufferers, who can fail altogether to impart some of its spirit.

Perhaps it will be said that this seems rather a secular way to talk about the Bible. You must get rid of all such prejudice. The chief trouble with every teacher is the difficulty of keeping his class interested in the Bible. The chief object, of course, is the spiritual teaching; but the story is the medium through which that teaching is given. Rousing the interest is but a preliminary to your main object of moving the heart; but it is an important—almost indispensable—preliminary. Be very sure that it is not waste of time to spend days in preparing to excite to the utmost the interest of your class. Be very sure that the more closely they are in sympathy with the story that God has inspired for them, the more likely they are to get hold of the spiritual teaching for which God inspired it.

II

Try to get a clear view of the circumstances and surroundings as you find them stated in ch. i. to iii. *v.* 6, which we may call the "Introduction to the Book."

The history proper begins at ch. iii. 7, and the Book would gain much in clearness by a division, or a broad, definite mark of some kind, just at that point. The Introduction (*i.e.*, ch. i. to iii. 6) states the position of things at the beginning of the history; and a very unsatisfactory position of things it is.

Probably, in reading of the conquest by Joshua, the class may have been so impressed by his success as to fancy the conquest entirely complete. If so, they get rather startled to find now the old inhabitants holding many of the strongest positions. As we reach ch. i. *vv.* 19-34, we find almost every tribe, instead of having completed the conquest of its lands, dwelling in the very midst of the enemy, and leaving in its hands most important strongholds. Turn back to Joshua (ch. xvi. 10 to xvii. 11-13, etc.). We find Joshua's campaign had given the tribes their allotted possessions, but it had left them to complete the conquest themselves by utterly driving out the defeated inhabitants. This they could have done, and they did not (see ch. i. 28-33 to ch. ii. 2). Hence the whole trouble. After Joshua's death they became corrupted and weakened in the midst of the idolators. There was no central authority when the old chief was gone; and a reign of anarchy and utter selfishness set in. It was a case of every tribe for itself, and every man doing that which was right in his own eyes; and the inevitable result followed, that in many cases the heathen grew strong, and regained the upper hand, and mightily oppressed Israel.

III

Now try to get right and sensible views about the heroes of the history. Do not try to show them up as faultless saints, or to ignore grave evil in their characters. But try to show God working in the midst of their evil, helping them to be better men, and strengthening them to do noble work. Show the good in them in so far as you can see it yourself, but no further. Above all things, be real in dealing with Scripture. Most certainly those rough, impulsive, passionate heroes did not possess all the virtues included in our high ideal of godliness.

But perhaps their very imperfections bring out the more clearly the virtues which they did possess— courage and self-sacrifice, and strong, deep faith in God. Show that God made allowances for the times in which they lived. Theirs was a dark and evil age. They had some teaching about religion, but very little as compared with us. They knew not of the higher teaching of Christ. They never heard or read the Sermon on the Mount; and, therefore, though we are quite right in condemning many of their actions, we must remember that they would have to be judged more gently than ourselves. "Many prophets and righteous men have desired to see the things which ye see, and have not seen them, and to hear the things which ye hear, and have not heard them."

IV

Last of all and most important of all impress upon yourself the main lesson of the Book, repeated in every fresh episode of oppression or deliverance:—

THE CHILDREN OF ISRAEL SINNED AGAINST THE LORD,
AND THE LORD DELIVERED THEM INTO THE HANDS OF
    THE ENEMY.
THEN THE CHILDREN OF ISRAEL CRIED UNTO THE LORD,
AND THE LORD RAISED THEM UP A DELIVERER.

Over and over again we go through that unvarying round of sinning, and punishment, and repenting, and deliverance, and sinning and punishment, and repenting and deliverance, till we can scarce help seeing the double lesson which, by means of it, the Israelites were intended to learn—that while the Lord our God is a jealous God, unfailingly punishing the wrong, yet the Lord our God is a merciful God, unfailingly forgiving "all them that are penitent."

I think it would be well, at the beginning of every Lesson, to make the class repeat and keep in mind this main lesson of the Book.

What is necessary to be said as to the moral difficulties has been already said in the Introduction to Lessons on Joshua.

LESSON I

SINNING AND PUNISHMENT, AND REPENTING AND DELIVERANCE

Judges II.

This is really a Lesson on the "Introduction of the Book" (ch. i. to iii. 6). It is more a preparation for the other Lessons than a Lesson itself; but the interest of the other Lessons will be considerably marred by any want of success in teaching this. Read carefully beforehand the "Lecture to the Teacher." It is mainly the substance of it that needs here to be taught.

The reasons for taking ch. ii. 1-7, as a retrospect of the historian, going back to Joshua's lifetime, will be found in any good commentary.

Read Chapter ii. We finished in last Lesson the story of Joshua and his wonderful conquest of western Palestine. All troubles seemed over. Victory, success, prosperity gained. *Now*, at the beginning of this Book, what do you think of the position of the people—prosperous? successful? victorious? happy? No. Why? What has happened? What had been the command, and how obeyed? (*v.* 2). (*Explain. Joshua's conquest not entirely complete. The tribes had each to complete it by driving out the conquered remnant, lest they should be corrupted by them. They were ordered to do so, and able to do so, but did not, and so got corrupted, and finally the old races began to get the upper hand, and mightily oppressed Israel. Teacher read* ch. i. 27-34. *Emphasize the disobedience. Point out in* v. 28 *that they preferred getting tribute to obeying God. Examine and comment on the whole of Chap.* ii.)

Now, all repeat these four words: SINNING, PUNISHMENT, REPENTING, DELIVERANCE. Everyone know them by heart? What first? Sinning. And after Sinning? And after Punishment? And after Repenting? Now, the whole story of the Book of Judges is about these four words. Every story is a story of these four words. Begin to-day with—

§ 1. Sinning

The history does not really begin until ch. iii. 7. All this previous part (ch. i. to iii. 6) is introductory, telling of the condition of the land and the people. (*Draw a pencil line in each pupil's Bible at end of* iii. 6.) In ch. i. the historian tells how they allowed the heathen to remain. And here, ch. ii., he is going back to tell of warning by an angel, even in Joshua's lifetime. What was it? How did the people receive it? Remember Joshua's warning, too, before he died? How they received it? (Joshua xxiv.)

97

Did they try to obey? How long? (*v.* 7). See the influence of a good man. Then what happened? (*v.* 10). How did evil begin? Not doing what God told them. What? Keep separate from and drive away the wicked natives. Throw down their altars and idols. Why? Why would a father tell his children to keep from bad company? Same reason here. God wanted Israelites to be good and holy, to preserve His teaching for all the world. If they got bad, could they help others to be good? Could you? Now see result. They stayed in the bad company, ate, and drank, and married with them, went to their idol feasts, worshipped idols, shared in their abominable sins, and forsook God (*v.* 12). Did God deserve to be forsaken? Be very careful about bad company. It may be pleasant at first; but it is grieving God, therefore you should keep clear of it. It will as surely defile you and make you bad, as it did the Israelites.

§ 2. Punishment

Now, our second word—what always follows sin? Punishment, God's displeasure. He hates sin with awful hatred. He is so pure and holy. He knows the misery and shame it brings on men, and how it separates them from Him. He must, if it be possible, drive men from it. Why? For His own advantage? No. For their good. If a father cannot keep his child from wrongdoing by love, what must he do? Punish. Ought he to punish? For his own good? No. So God has attached certain punishments to sin. If a child has the habit of stealing or lying, what is God's punishment? No one will trust him.

If he neglects to learn? Spoils his future. So other sins. Besides other punishment, there is always the pain of conscience, like God's rod, to make you smart for wrong. (*Explain what conscience is—help them to realize. See Lesson on Achan.*) Why does God attach punishment to sin? How punished Israelites? Took away His help from them—left them to themselves. The Canaanites conquered them, and oppressed them—awful suffering. Do you think they deserved it? Why?

§ 3. Repenting

What after punishment? Then they were very wretched (*v.* 15). Greatly distressed. They were taxed, and robbed, and murdered. Farmer grew crops and reared cattle—then taken by force from him. No pity for them—they had to hide in caves and dens—utterly crushed, no friend, no helper. Whose fault? Yes. They had forsaken their great Friend and Helper, and He had to let them suffer for their own good.

At last, in their utter misery they cry out to Him. (See ch. iii. 9, 15, etc.) Sometimes only misery makes sinners do that, *e.g.*, Prodigal Son. One reason of the world's misery, to make people cry to God. Israelites wretched: no one else to cry to. So they try in despair if God will hear. "O God, forgive us, we are ashamed to ask—we have been very bad—we deserve nothing but punishment—but we have no one else to come to, and we are awfully miserable!" Did they deserve that God should hear? But, oh! He *is* good. There is no limit to the loving-kindness of God.

What comes after repenting? Repeat the four words again.

§ 4. Deliverance

God cannot bear to let them suffer. "Like as a father pitieth." (Psalms ciii. 13). You know how father or mother would feel if child were in terrible pain. Even if it were child's own fault. God is better than any father or mother. His heart is sore for us even when He makes us suffer. And if we only turn and cry to Him, and ask Him to help us and make us good, He tells us what He will do. What? Remember Prodigal Son. Now, see *v.* 16. He delivered them, and, perhaps, He hoped they would keep their promise now, and try to be good. Did they? (*v.* 17). Oh, how many disappointments God gets. People say, "O God, help me, and I'll try to be good." Sometimes they do. Great pleasure to God. Often they do not. Great disappointment to Him. If people treated a man—a king on earth—like that, would he not be very angry? Would he ever help them again? Oh! we never can understand how wonderfully good God is. Again they sinned, and He punished them, and again they cried out in sorrow and pain, and He delivered them. Over, and over, and over again, until anybody but God would have been utterly disgusted and enraged with them. But he never tired of waiting and helping. That is just like God always. That was why our Saviour died for us, though we deserved to die. He could not bear to let us.

"For the love of God is broader than the limits of man's mind
And the heart of the Eternal is most wonderfully kind."

Now, learn this TWO-FOLD LESSON of the Book of Judges. We shall want to say it by heart before each of the Lessons following. It belongs to all of them.

TWO-FOLD LESSON

The Children of Israel Sinned, and were Punished.
The Children of Israel Repented, and were Delivered.

QUESTIONS FOR LESSON I

Repeat the two-fold lesson which gives the central teaching of this book.

Show how this same thing is true nowadays.

Why, do you think, does God attach punishment to sin?

If Joshua had already conquered Palestine why all this fighting now?

What do you think of these heroes in the Book of Judges?

Point out the good and the evil in their characters.

What allowance should we make for them?

Could we Christians make such allowance for bad in ourselves? Why not?

FOUR DELIVERANCES

Judges III. 7-15, and v. 31; IV. 1-15.

The main subject of Lesson is the Battle of Mount Tabor—Only rough outline here, but the teacher who is capable of enthusiasm over his subject could make it a most thrilling lesson. Use map. A rough penciled plan of the battle, where possible, would add to the interest. Consult Stanley's *Jewish Church*, and Thomson's *The Land and the Book.* Show the river Kishon, and the mountain streams that led to the catastrophe.

The storm of rain is not directly mentioned. Josephus tells of it (*Antiquities of the Jews* v. 5, § 4). Deborah, in ch. v. 20-22, exults that the heavens and the stars had fought against Sisera; and her graphic picture of the swelling river and the plunging horses makes it a very probable explanation.

With senior classes teach more fully the closing thought in Lesson, God's gradual progressive Revelation. It will be a great help in the moral difficulties of Old Testament.

Remember last Lesson? What was state of the Israelites? Whose fault was it? How? Now each of the class repeat carefully the "Two-fold Lesson of the Book." *(See end of last Lesson.)* To-day we have four examples of this. (1) OTHNIEL. (Teacher read iii. 7-11: notice how soon after Joshua's death, see ch. i. 13.) (2) EHUD. Read iii. 12-16, then very briefly sketch the story: compare his raising the people, *vv.* 27, 28, with Alfred the Great raising the Saxons in time of Danish rule. (3) SHAMGAR. Know nothing of him except ch. v. 6. (4) DEBORAH, now to be discussed in ch. iv.—Now whole class together repeat the "Two-fold Lesson," as above, and name these first four deliverers. From what nations did each deliver?

§ 1. *Deborah*

To-day story of Deborah. Remark that ch. iv. and v. are the same story in prose and poetry. (Read ch. iv.; try by a few passing comments to keep the connection clear, and keep up the interest while reading. Then go back to the beginning of chapter.) How often already the sinning and repenting? Now it is all beginning again. From whom had Ehud delivered? How long did they keep right? Who was new oppressor? Was he powerful? (*v.* 3). Ever hear of Jabin and of his famous chariots before? (Joshua xi. Chariots, *vv.* 4 and 9.) What Jabin's position then? and now? He mightily oppressed (*v.* 3); see ch. v. 6, 7, 8. People had to hide in the hills and forests, dared not go on public road—would be killed, robbed, ill-treated. (See last Lesson.) Terrible trouble again, had brought it all on themselves. What do? (*v.* 3). Yes, only when in trouble they cried to Him. How wonderful that He should still listen, that He should not have been utterly wearied of them! See how He delivered them.

Ever hear in English history of King Charles' Oak? Here we have Deborah's Palm tree. A great, good woman, great influence. Cases brought to be tried by her. Think of her years of anxious thought—of prayer— of advice and warning to the many who came to her—of comforting and encouraging them to trust in their God. She was a prophetess teaching them about Jehovah. At last she began to see that the time of deliverance was near. How? Perhaps God taught it to her. Perhaps she saw great sorrow and repentance, and crying to God everywhere, and knew that He would surely hear. At any rate, she began rousing the people. Very like Joan of Arc, in France.—France helpless, nearly conquered, King and generals had given up; but Joan, a poor, praying girl, roused them to high excitement of patriotism, and won many battles. The soldiers would do anything for her. Wonderful what earnestness and enthusiasm and faith can do. The people crowded to Deborah (ch. v. 9, 13, 14, 15). From Zebulun, from Naphtali, the warriors gathered in—the chiefs of Issachar, the bands of Ephraim and Manasseh, the crowding troops of Benjamin, rich and poor, high and low, "they that sat on rich carpets of state"—"they that humbly walked by the way," all crowding on to the great muster-place of Mount Tabor. High enthusiasm and courage and hope—a little before in their terror they dare not face a Canaanite, dare not walk on highway. But now Deborah was with them, and they knew God was with Deborah. She had sent for the great warrior Barak, to lead them, and eagerly they looked forward to battle with the foe.

§ 2. *The Battle of Mount Tabor*

Soon Sisera heard of the rising. He dwelt where? (*v.* 2). Harosheth of the Gentiles, which probably means the Factory or Forge-place of the Peoples, perhaps where the great iron chariots were made. He determined to crush rebellion at once. Out from Harosheth swept his mighty host, his prancing horses, his 900 chariots—a grand array, with banners and spears they swept along the plain. On the plain was the best place for chariots to fight. Therefore Israel kept to the hills. Beside the river Kishon he pitched his camp. Israelites watching on the hills. They see the river running by the camp, and the mountain-streams running to the river, and the great host of warriors beside them. Dare they come down within reach of these terrible chariots?

Suddenly the sky darkens, clouds break, rain pours. All day long the driving rain continues. Ha! in a moment Deborah sees it. The river is rising, the streams are swelling: soon the whole plain will be flooded and soft. "Up, up!" she cries to Barak; "sweep down on the foe. The Lord has delivered Sisera into thy hands!" And down he charged with his 10,000 warriors. No longer any dread of the terrible chariots; the horses were plunging madly; the chariots were sinking in the soft ground; the river was rising; the foe was defeated before ever the warriors of Barak got down. Listen to Deborah's shout of exultation (ch. v. 21, 22):—

> "The torrent of Kishon swept them away,
>   The ancient torrent, the torrent of Kishon,
>   'Mid the stamping of the hoofs of their horses,
>   In the plungings and the plungings of their mighty ones."

An interesting illustration is the other battle of Mount Tabor, A.D. 1799, where many of the Turkish soldiers were drowned and swept off by the Kishon.

Awful and utter was the ruin of Canaanites. So complete that centuries afterwards it was remembered in the national hymns as the terrible destruction of Endor (see Psalms lxxxiii. 9, 10).

Israel was completely delivered again. By whom? Deborah? Barak? The Israelite soldiers? No, by God, who used them. See Deborah's own opinion (ch. v. 2, 3). They did their part—that is how God usually works—by means of men. But they were weak and untrained—without proper weapons (ch. v. 8)—cowed by long years of oppression—dared not even walk on the highways openly (*v.* 6), much less attack their mighty Canaanite masters. But they had cried unto the Lord; and with Him on their side weakness did not matter. See Hebrews xi. 34. Out of weakness made strong, etc. Remember it is not only in Bible history such things happen. The Reformation; the abolition of the slave-trade; the crusade against drunkenness, etc. A few weak men had to fight overwhelming odds; but the odds did not matter. God was with them. They could not fail to conquer. In your school life or business life there may be a mighty evil. Bad tone in school, lying and dishonourable conduct, etc. You feel it hopeless to try to put it right. Do not be hopeless. It is God's battle, not yours. Get one or two to be on your side. Let them get others. Pray—strive—be enthusiastic about it, like Deborah, and you, too, must win. Let that be your rule in all your life, and God will fight with you, and make the world purer, and brighter, and happier, by means of you.

§ 3. Jael and Sisera

Only just time to say a few words about Sisera. He fled out of his entangled chariot to the tent of Jael. She, too, hated the oppressor, and sympathized with the poor Israelites. And so, when he was fast asleep in her tent, she stole softly and drove the great tent pin through his skull. Was it a good act or evil? *Try to get the honest judgment of the child's conscience.* Well, it was partly good and greatly evil; and we must make much allowance for the evil because of the ignorance. It would be a very wicked thing for us to do, because we know God's will more perfectly. She was but a poor ignorant Arab woman. She knew no better. She had not the teaching of our Lord, as we have. And because she, in her ignorance, meant to do good for the oppressed Israelites, and risked her life to destroy the oppressors and because she did not see the wrong, all allowance must be made for her. If anybody, honestly intending to do God's will, does in mistake that which is not God's will, God will make a great deal of allowance for his ignorance. God's kind grace will disentangle the good from the evil in the mingled web of our service. If Jael had known the teaching of Christ, as we do, her act would have been a wicked, unpardonable treachery. If Deborah had known the teaching of Christ, she could never have blessed or approved of the deed. But they lived in dark times of imperfect knowledge of God. The world like a great school—God's teaching gradual, as men could bear it. Jael and Deborah were only in the lower classes of the great school of God, but were doing their best in their lower class. (See next Lesson for fuller treatment of the blessing on Jael.)

QUESTIONS FOR LESSON II

Repeat again the two-fold lesson.

Who were oppressing Israel now?

Name of the great battle in this lesson?

Who were: (1) Deborah, (2) Barak, (3) Sisera, (4) Jael?

Try to make word-picture of the battle of Mt. Tabor.

(a) The rising of oppressed Israel.

(b) The coming of Sisera.

(c) The enemy's army on plains.

(d) The storm.

(e) Barak and his men charging down upon the foe.

Why did the enemy keep on the plains?

How did the great rainstorm destroy this advantage?

Who really delivered Israel?

LESSON III

DEBORAH'S SONG OF PRAISE

Judges V.

It is almost impossible for any teacher really to do justice to this splendid ode, so vividly dramatic—so full of passion, and fire, and high poetic genius. But if the teacher will study it deeply, and try to enter into its spirit, until it lays hold of him, and rouses him to *feel*—then, even if he cannot express the half of his feelings, he will, at least, make the class feel in some degree too. It seems best to divide the songs into sections for teaching, *e.g.:*—I. The Prelude of Thanksgiving to God, who has roused the leaders, and has delivered from such misery (*vv.* 1-8). II. The Gathering of the Heroes (*vv.* 8-19). III. The Recreants (*vv.* 16-18). IV. The Battle and the Flight (*vv.* 19-23). V. The Blessing of Jael (*vv.* 24-31). Indicate this division as you read. I should advise that this chapter be read *by the teacher* for the class; otherwise there is danger that much of the spirit and vivid colouring of the poem will be lost. If possible, use the Revised Version, where it is printed as poetry. Tell the children your divisions and the titles of them as you read.

With regard to the Blessing of Jael, with all who are old enough to understand it, and to feel the recoil of conscience against it, teach it carefully and deliberately. Don't speak of any moral difficulty in it. Simply criticize the words of Jael and the blessing by Deborah as you would the acts and the words of Gideon, or Jephthah, or Samson. Be especially careful not to leave the impression that the Bible declares God's approval and blessing of an act from which the conscience of almost every child old enough to understand it will probably recoil.

The main lessons of the Song are—The duty of thanksgiving; the nobleness of self-sacrifice; and the meanness and wrong of selfish indifference. Especially be careful to close with the thought of Him who was the grandest example of self-sacrifice for others.

§ 1. *Thanksgiving*

Remind and question briefly about previous Lesson leading up to the thought of what God had accomplished. Ask, who accomplished the deliverance? Deborah? Barak? What did they themselves think? (*v.* 2). And so they recognized duty of thanking God for it. They thanked Him for the avenging of Israel; for the willingness of the people; for the old deliverance of Israel from Egypt (*vv.* 4, 5); for the rescuing of the poor and oppressed now from their wretchedness (*vv.* 6-8). And their thankfulness so great that they wanted all to learn it. Made a stirring song—most effective way of teaching—sung before the army—all soon learnt it. Remember a similar thing before? (Exodus xv.) Deborah calls on the people to—what? (*v.* 2). Sets example herself (*v.* 3). She goes on praising the courage, the patriotism, the faithfulness of the people; but (see *v.* 9) it is all something to thank God for. God is everything to her. All good comes from Him. All the good in men was put in their hearts by Him. Praise the Lord, she sings; bless ye the Lord for it all. See that spirit through the psalms. What do we learn first from Deborah's song? Thanksgiving. We have all so many things to thank God for. Tell me some. Health, home, father, mother, food, clothes, play, friends. Remember all are God's gifts— *e.g.* harvest. Ten seeds put in the ground and covered. Farmer goes away. Finds 100 when he comes to harvest time. Where did the other ninety come from? Point out our utter dependence. Every harvest the world within a few months of starvation; could not live six months if God kept back His gift one year. What would it be if God forgot it all, or kept it all back for one year? But He does not. He never forgets us. "Oh, that men would therefore praise the Lord for His goodness, and declare the wonders that He doeth for the children of men." (Psalms cvii. 15). Health, and strength, and happiness, and home, and friends, and all the blessings of this life, are God's gifts, and, above all, His inestimable love, in the redemption of the world. Yet we seldom thank Him. We can thank anybody else but God, and love anybody else when good to us. We don't trouble to thank God. It would pain us to be so treated. Does it not pain God? Deborah will not pain Him thus. With glad heart she leads the people to offer their earnest thanks to Him.

§ 2. The Gathering of the Heroes

vv. 8-16

But she is glad and thankful also for the heroes who left their homes and farms to fight for their nation. Who? (*vv.* 14, 15, 18). There are always brave, unselfish men who will risk much for God and for their neighbours. These came with their lives in their hands. Who puts in us the thoughts and impulses of courage and self-sacrifice? The Holy Spirit. So Deborah thanks God, but also is full of admiration for the men who "jeoparded their lives to the death." Does God care much whether we are brave and unselfish? Can you follow example of Deborah's heroes? How? Battle? Perhaps so, by-and-by. But now? He who does things unpleasant to him for others' sake. Who bears being laughed at when he could escape it. *Teacher can easily explain and illustrate, keeping in mind that self-sacrifice is the quality that gives nobleness to such acts. Tell of the heroism and self-sacrifice in the terrible fight with Germany. Especially try to help to manly thoughts of religion—that daring and self-sacrifice are grand in God's sight.*

§ 3. The Recreants

vv. 16, 17, 23

But all are not heroes. The warrior prophetess has no words too strong to express her indignant contempt for the selfish, cowardly, sneaking creatures who "came not to the help of the Lord against the mighty." Name them. Why not come? Cared more for their own wretched little selves. Reuben, after doubting and hesitating, stayed where he was, and left his brethren to fight and die without him. Gilead thought about their flocks and their pastures; Dan and Asher about their ships, and fishing, and merchandise. There are always the selfish and indifferent, to whom gain and worldly interest are higher things than duty and nobleness. There are always boys and girls who will not help another or share with another. Always men and women who care only for pleasure and money, and let the heathen abroad, and the poor destitute at home, shift for themselves as they can. The Lord wants all their help against the mighty sins and sorrows of life; but they care only for self. They "come not to the help of the Lord," etc. (*v.* 23). Repeat Deborah's awful words about them (*v.* 23). How utterly God hates that sin of selfish indifference. There are few sins worse than that.

§ 4. *The Blessing of Jael*

Even Jael, with her brave, cruel deed, seems grand in comparison with these selfish cowards. Cursed shall they be (*v.* 23); but blessed shall she be who, alone and unaided, with her weak woman's hand, accomplished that in which they so shamefully failed. She ran terrible risk for herself, and her family. She dared much for no gain to herself, but to deliver Israel from the tyrant's yoke; and there was much in that to praise her for. Even in recent times, in the terrible days of the French Revolution, when a fierce, brutal tyrant was sending hundreds of innocent people to the scaffold, a brave woman, Charlotte Corday, determined to rid her country of his presence, and at the cost of her life crept stealthily into his house and stabbed him in his bath. No one blames her. Many praise her. But are we bound to give our approval to Jael's act? No. Does the Bible say that God blessed her for it? No. What does it say? That Deborah, a great warrior queen, like Boadicea of old, blessed her for her courage and self-sacrifice. Deborah was a great and noble woman, and even a prophetess who taught the people. God used her and helped her like the other Judges, and delivered Israel by means of her; but she lived in dark times, of imperfect knowledge of God; and in her enthusiastic admiration of Jael's courage and self-sacrifice she did not see the evil in Jael's deed.

Try to close by briefly recalling the main lessons of the chapter: I. The duty of thanksgiving. II. The grandeur of self-sacrifice for the sake of others. Close with this question:—For what is our greatest thanksgiving due? and Who is the grandest example of self-sacrifice for others? Ah! He did not think about Himself or His own comfort. He never thought of that from cradle to cross. He laid down His beautiful, self-forgetting life for the sake of the very people who pursued Him to His death.

QUESTIONS FOR LESSON III

Is this chapter prose or poetry?

Who composed it?

Who did she think had delivered Israel?

How do you know? (*v.* 2)

How does she praise the heroes who fought for God and their country?

Did all fight who ought? Why?

What does the song say of them?

Repeat the verse, "Curse ye Meroz," etc.

What does it teach in our day?

What did Jael do? Was it right or wrong or both? Explain.

GIDEON—CALLED OF GOD

Judges VI.

This chapter is too long for the class to read. Teacher should read it pretty rapidly for them, dividing it for easier comprehension into sections—1. The Oppressors (*vv.* 1-7). 2. The Prophet (*vv.* 7-11). 3. The Angel's Message (*vv.* 11-25). 4. The Reformer (*vv.* 25-33). 5. The Deliverer (*vv.* 33-40). Explanation about Midian (*vv.* 1-7) should be brief, but forcible and clear.

§ 1. The Oppression

Repeat again the "Two-Fold Lesson." Exemplified again (*v.* 1). Who oppressors now? Yes. These Arabian tribes, with two kings, Zebah and Zalmunna (ch. viii. 5), two chiefs, Oreb and Zeeb—*i.e.*, Raven and Wolf (ch. vii. 25). *Illustrate from names in Indian tribes. Fine opportunity of vivid word-pictures. Arab tribes of the desert, fleet Arab horses and camels, countless hosts, like locusts in the valley* (ch. vii. 12). Great splendour of robes and gold ornaments (ch. viii. 26). Awful

117

tyranny, not only wanted the plunder, but hated Israel with deadly hatred. Why? Ever hear of them before? (Numbers xxii. 7, xxv., especially *vv.* 17, 18; xxxi. 7, 8). Yes, Balaam could not curse Israel for them; but he showed them how to make Israel do wrong, and God punished Israel awfully for it; and then they in return warred against Midian, and nearly destroyed them.

So Midian hated them greatly, and oppressed them terribly. How long? (*v.* 1). What did they do? Every year at harvest-time crowded in to seize the harvests and the cattle, and the wretched Israelites were starving. Did they resist? What did they do? (*v.* 2). Yes, hid themselves like rats in their holes. Why so afraid? Were they not as many as in Deborah's time, when they conquered the Canaanites? Why so afraid now? Because they had sinned against God till they had lost His approval and His help. That is what makes cowards. That is what takes the heart and enthusiasm out of men. What is the only hope in such a case? (*v.* 6). Year after year passed. Seven harvests were plundered. And then at last they cried unto the Lord. How could they presume to do it after treating God so? They had learned one thing, at least—that though God hated sin, and had to punish terribly, yet He was always longing to see them repent and be forgiven.

§ 2. *The Prophet*

Repeat again the Two-Fold Lesson. What always came after the "crying unto the Lord"? A deliverer. Was it so now? Who was sent? Why not deliverer at *once* sent? Because God sends not always what we *wish*, but what we *need*. Perhaps people not yet ready—not sorry enough for their sin. Not see their sin at all, only their misery. What was the message? "Look how good God has been to you, and how often you have disappointed Him." Just what everyone should say who is not living for God. "How good God has been to me, made me, preserved me, loved me, died for me, invited me to be His child, and enter into His heaven. And yet I have been disappointing Him continually. What a shame!"

§ 3. God's Plan

But God was preparing deliverer, too. Amongst the poor, trampled Israelites was one man, a brave soldier (*v.* 12), whose heart was very sore for the troubles of his people. His name? He had to flee like the rest, and try to hide what he could of his harvest. Down hidden in the wine-press he was threshing his father's wheat, and brooding over his people's misery and raging in his heart against the tyranny of their oppressors (*see v.* 13). Suddenly he is conscious of a mysterious presence under the oak before him. The Bible keeps always before us the great kindly spirit-world interested in our world and surrounding it as the ocean surrounds the land. And messages from that world come with messages to this world as so evidently shown in the life of our Lord. Gideon hears the strange salutation. "The Lord is with thee, thou mighty man of valour." "Oh, how can the Lord be with us? He has cast us off." Poor, hopeless, despondent Gideon, with the black, miserable outlook for his nation before him. And then comes thrilling through him the rousing word from the Lord: "Go in this thy might. Thou shalt save Israel. Have not I sent thee?" In his wonder and humility he pleads: "How shall I save?" Like Moses (Exodus iii. 11). And in reply gets the word which was such a source of courage to Moses, to Joshua, to all who have ever done great things for God: "Certainly I will be with thee." You remember what great things Joshua did in the strength of that promise. A man can do almost anything if he feels that God is with him—that he is on the side of God and right.

§ 4. *The Reformer*

Soon Gideon had need of this help and encouragement. Was he commissioned at once to go out and deliver his nation? No. What then? (*v.* 25). Why? The trouble had come on Israel by reason of their Idolatry. "You must be a Reformer first," said God. "And you must begin at home. Your own town has an altar of Baal, the filthy god of the Canaanites. It is in the high rock in your own father's grounds. Your own family worship it. That must be dashed down at once." Think of the daring needed for that in a town full of idolators. Why, they would tear a man in pieces if he dared to touch it. Did Gideon hesitate? Did he know the danger of it? What gave this courage to the man who had to hide in a winepress a few days before? Repeat again God's promise to him. Ah, that was the secret. And so cautiously, but fearlessly, he laid his plans. The people, as usual, went to their beds that night without a suspicion. Next morning a startling sight on the hill. The whole town gaze in horror. Then wild uproar, shouts, and yells of rage in the streets. "Our altar is thrown down, our idol is broken and burned in the fire. Who has dared to commit this awful thing in our town?" Like the day when Luther burned the Papal Bull. Like the night of the Placards in French Huguenot story. In the morning through every town in France every man as he went out saw a staring placard attacking the corruption of the Church. Fierce indignation and stern search for the perpetrators. So in Abiezer. Backward and forward surged the gathering crowd. Who hath done this thing? Then with a shout they rush towards the house of Joash. "Gideon, thy son, hath broken down the altar of our god. Bring him out, bring him out, that he may die for his crime." You remember the clever, quiet reply of Joash? (*v.* 31). Yes, just the argument against all idolatry to-day. If he be a god, let him plead for himself. He who could not save himself from Gideon, how can he save anybody else? What do we learn from this order to Gideon? That none of us is fit to help on God's work in the world till we have first set ourselves right with Him. If we are allowing any sins in our own life they must be first attacked.

§ 5. *The Deliverer*

Gideon nearly paid with his life for his boldness in reform. But he dared it all for the sake of God and righteousness. And now there is a still more daring deed to be done. It is just the harvest time, when the fierce

121

Midianites crowd in like locusts to carry off the poor farmers' crops. As usual, they come in their insolent pride, expecting the people to run off to their hiding-holes. Ah, but there is a change! The power of God's strength, the enthusiasm for heroic deeds, has come strongly upon Gideon. Already he has startled the whole country around by his daring attack on the altar. Now they hear strange, almost incredible, rumours. A brave stand is to be made. The trumpet of Gideon is ringing out through the hills, and all Abiezer is gathering after him! The bravery of one man raised the bravery of many. And, as in the days of Deborah, the enthusiasm spread. Through all the country round sped the messengers of the chief, through Manasseh, through Asher, through Zebulun, and Naphtali. Oh, the delight and eagerness of the people. God with us again! A deliverer again! Every day his numbers increased, until at last, with an army of 32,000 men at his back, he set out to deliver his country from the foe. We shall see in next Lesson the extraordinary way in which nearly all that great army melted away without striking a blow.

We have now to close our Lesson by reminding ourselves again of the secret of the wonderful power that had come to Gideon. Why could he dare to risk his life in destroying the idol? Because he knew God was with him. Why did his heart swell with courage and enthusiasm and willingness to sacrifice all for the sake of his people? Because of the conviction that God was with him. Remember that is the one great secret of strength. That conviction is the secret of power in every man who has accomplished wonders for God.

Can we have that conviction too? How can we get it? How shall we use that strength when we do get it? In living brave, true lives for God. In being in very deed Christ's faithful soldiers and servants to our lives' end. By always getting on to the side of right. Whenever we are choosing the right as far as we know it, we can feel sure that we have God at our back to help us.

QUESTIONS FOR LESSON IV

Repeat again the two-fold lesson.

Who were the oppressors now?

Israel had a terrible experience of that nation in Balaam's time. What was it?

Who was the new deliverer raised up by God?

Tell of his first appearance as a reformer.

Tell of his first appearance as deliverer.

Repeat his battle cry.

LESSON V

GIDEON—THE SWORD OF THE LORD

Judges VII.

Recapitulate briefly last Lesson. Try to get feelings roused in pity for the down-trodden Israelites, in sympathy with the heroic purpose of Gideon. (In all cases of battle or slaughter where God's approval is indicated, try to find and show the reason. Either some oppression to be hindered or some great cause of righteousness to be furthered.) Gideon's heart is beating high with hope. "God is with me. His Angel has been sent to me. The signs I prayed for have been granted me. Now I am going to do great things for God and for my people—break down all altars, reform religion, crush the pride of the cruel chiefs of Midian. I am, by the help of God, to bring great blessing to my native land!"

Then read the chapter quickly through, dividing it into sections. Section 1. First testing (*vv.* 1-4). Section 2. Second testing (*vv.* 4-9). Section 3. Gideon's sign (*vv.* 9-15). Section 4. The battle of Jezreel (*v.* 15 to end). Name the sections, and watch carefully to keep up the interest by a passing remark as they read.

§ 1. God's Choosing

Read Sections 1 and 2 taken together. Picture Gideon—proud, glad, enthusiastic: a few months ago so insignificant—hiding from Midian, and now a great leader, with 32,000 behind him, and the army of the oppressor on the valley before him. Think of a man at such a time being told, Your great army must disband without striking a blow. Surely it must have startled him. Yet he felt that God must be right.

Why was army reduced? (*v.* 2). Yes, they must be made to feel that they were only God's instruments— this is what must rouse awe, and wonder, and trust, and thanksgiving in the heart of the nation. What was first test? How many went? How many remained? Seemed a very small army now to meet the countless hosts of Midian. How is their vast number described? (*v.* 12). Yet even 10,000 too many. What was the next test? How would this test them so as to keep the best? Picture the host of Midian watching the strange manœuvres. See 22,000 throw down arms and go home. See 10,000 drawn up on bank of stream. Suddenly 9,700 throw themselves on their faces, completely off guard—no self-control, no watchfulness—exposing themselves perhaps to a quick charge of Midian from behind. But here and there along the lines a man stood, steady, restrained, on his guard, stooping quickly to dip his hand for water, and rising alert in his place again. How many such? Yes. In the whole army there were but 300 heroes of courage, and self-denial, and watchfulness fit for God's great work. What heroes they were! They had to stand still before the countless hosts of the enemy, and see 9,700 march away. And these 300 had to dare all for God. (Read Tennyson's *The Charge of the Light Brigade*.) By these 300 choice men God said He would deliver Israel? Why were these special men chosen for God's work? Was it chance? Was there any reason? They were the best, choicest, fittest, most heroic, and therefore, God used them. Which will do best work for God—100 careless, half-hearted, or ten enthusiastic, out-and-out Christians, eager to sacrifice everything for God and right?

That is where Israelite history differs from all other history. They never claim any victory or achievement as their own. God must teach Israel in order that Israel should teach to all mankind man's utter dependence on God for all good.

§ 2. The Battle of the Pitchers

Now let us see what these chosen men had to do. How anxious Gideon and they when they stood alone, only 300 against many thousands. What was their comfort? They had obeyed God, and, therefore, they could trust Him to take care of them. Did God give further encouragement? Picture the sleeping hosts, the active Israelite chief creeping cautiously from rock to rock into their midst. The dream about the cake of barley bread rolling on and overthrowing the tent. Meaning? Barley bread, the cheap bread of the poor, meant Gideon and his 300; they seemed such a contemptible thing, like a loaf of the common brown bread, scorned by the proud Arabs. How glad Gideon was. It was God's sign to him. What did he do at once? (*v.* 15). Worshipped and thanked God, and went back full of hope to the soldiers.

Now see the clever stratagem. The 300 are prepared. Torches covered by a little jar in one hand, and in the other a trumpet. Watch them stealthily surrounding the sleeping army—all perfectly still—all perfectly dark. Now intense excitement—wait for signal. Suddenly Gideon's trumpet rings out, and with one blow his pitcher is smashed. In an instant 300 blows smash 300 pitchers, and 300 trumpets ring out in the night, and 300 voices in every direction shout in fierce excitement the war-cry of their leader—"For the Lord, and for Gideon!" What next? Did the 300 fight? (*v.* 21). No. They stood still. They had trusted God. They had risked their lives. And now God justified their trust. In frenzied panic the sleepers sprang up. The darkness all around them was full of sounding trumpets, and flashing lights, and ringing war-cries. There was a terrified stampede. Every man slashed all round him. Friends fought with friends, and all that could flee fled for their lives. And so the terrible misery of Israel was removed, and the fierce, cruel oppressor had his power broken for ever. And all this was done by God. But done by means of the 300 heroes whom He had specially tested and chosen to accomplish this great deliverance.

§ 3. God's Work in the World

Does God want any great work done in the world to-day? Does any testing like that of Gideon's men take place in the world to-day? Yes, always. Every day. Are you surprised at this? Think of any great work for God in the world. Just look at beginning of Christianity. How many followed Christ to hear Him? He had twice to feed them—how many? Yes, many thousands followed him. What did He want followers to do? To make the world better. Were all these fit? No, large numbers got tired and went away, like Gideon's 22,000. Were all the rest earnest enough to do much good? No, He had still to sift them. He picked out seventy disciples to go teaching, and twelve apostles to rouse workers and teachers everywhere. Why were these seventy and twelve especially chosen? Because, like Gideon's 300, they were the fittest, the most earnest.

Look on the world to-day. Christ is still wanting great work to be done—wanting hero soldiers to fight His enemies of drunkenness, and dishonesty, and lying, and sin of every kind. He wants people to give up friends and home for sake of His poor heathen children. How many in this school and parish are pledged to be His soldiers? All of us in Baptism were pledged, "to be Christ's faithful soldier and servant to his life's end." But are all earnest and loyal and fit to do God's work, to conquer sin in the world, and make the world better, purer, happier? No. First, the large number who don't care at all about God's work, like Gideon's 22,000. Then there remain those who *do* care, but not very earnestly. They say their prayers each day, and come to church and Sunday-school, but do not think much about the brave true life that God looks for. They are not loving God and right *very* much. They are not fighting *hard* for Christ's sake against temper and laziness, etc. They are like the 10,000 remaining to Gideon. Do they do anything to make world better? Yes, a little. But they are fit to do much? Suppose carelessness and lying and bad words go on. God wants it put right. Can He use them? Not much. Whom does He use? The few who are earnest, who are longing to do right, and to serve and please God—the few who are willing to bear being unpopular and being laughed at by companions for the sake of God. They are like Gideon's 300 whom God chose to do great things for Him. *E.g.*, one boy who has the courage to kneel at his prayers has shamed a whole roomful into doing it. One man or woman who has the courage to stand alone against evil companions or evil customs. Pray to God to make you fit to do great things for Him, not by talking or boasting or fault-finding, but by living a brave, true, faithful life yourself, and thus helping others in the path to right. And thus you will be training yourself to do great, good work in the world for God.

QUESTIONS FOR LESSON V

Gideon's great army had to be reduced. Why?

Tell of first testing of the men.

Tell of the second testing.

Anything like this happening in God's work in the world to-day?

Picture in words the Battle of the Pitchers.

What was the secret of Gideon's courage and power?

LESSON VI

JEPHTHAH—
IGNORANCE OF GOD

Judges XI.

Divide the chapter for better comprehension into three sections: (1) The Coming of Jephthah (*vv.* 1-12). (2) The Controversy with Ammon (*vv.* 13-29). (3) Jephthah's Vow (*vv.* 29-40). Some people shrink from the view taken in this Lesson that Jephthah actually offered up his daughter as a human sacrifice. But human sacrifice would not at all revolt the people at that time. In *v.* 31 he says, *I will offer it for a burnt offering*, and in *v.* 39 he did with her *according to his vow*.

§ 1. *Jephthah*

Here is another story of another deliverance in some other time and place.

Read Section 1. In order to keep up the connection with the "Two-Fold Lesson," look back to ch. x., and

131

read *vv.* 6, 7, 15. Here we have same old story—Sinning, Punishment, Repenting, Deliverance. Who were oppressors? Who the new deliverer? What do you think of him? Was he as good as Gideon? See ch. viii. 23. Now read xi. 9. One thought only of his country's good; the other thought much of his own position and advantage. But Jephthah had had a hard life: not as easy for him to be good and unselfish. Driven out of his home when young, a fugitive, an exile, a leader of a band of robbers. Ought he to be judged as sharply as we? God makes allowances for men's disadvantages. So, we see, his tribe, who had turned him out, came pleading to him again. And he came back to lead Israel. And God accepted him, and helped him to conquer. (See *v.* 29.)

Read Section 2, *vv.* 12-29. Did he at once begin to fight? What did he do? Do you think it was a good plan to begin by remonstrating? Do you remember our Lord's advice, "Tell him his fault between thee and him alone"? Did you ever know of a quarrel between two boys or two girls, or two families? Do you think if they had talked it over together in a friendly way, and tried to find out each other's feelings, it would have been better? In disagreement with another, we should always try to be fair with him. Try to "put yourself in his place." Try to understand him. Say to him, "I don't want to be unfair or unkind; please tell me exactly where you think I am wrong; let us try to understand each other." One very good rule is: always try to look for the faults in yourself, and to look for excuses for the other. If both would do that, God would be pleased, and the quarrel would soon be ended. However, in Jephthah's case, the two parties could not agree, and so had to fight, and Jephthah and his men conquered by the help of God.

§2. Jephthah's Vow

Read *vv.* 29-40. We saw that Jephthah was not a very good man. Is not *v.* 29 a strange one, then? Explain here that the Spirit of the Lord bestows various gifts, according to men's natural differences, and according to the needs of the men or of their times. The spirit of holiness, of love, of understanding, and of common-sense. Here the gift seems especially the gift of energy and power for his great work. See this more fully in Samson afterwards. True, every help from God's Spirit makes men better and nobler. But every help from Him does not make them absolutely good and noble at once. A man may be rash or foolish or mistaken, or even weak in yielding to temptation, and yet may be receiving help from the Spirit of the Lord. No doubt, Jephthah was made a braver and a stronger chieftain, and a better man, by the help of God's Spirit; but many faults still remained in him. What a strange ignorance of God in his famous vow!

What is a vow? What was his vow? (*vv.* 30-31). What did it mean? That he would offer up a human sacrifice to God. Was it right to do that? Would God like it? No! it would be horrible to God. But poor Jephthah did not know that. He had been an exile in Syria—a robber chief—and had the usual superstition of Syria about human sacrifices. The people about him offered up their children to Moloch, their god, when they wanted victory. The Carthaginians sacrificed a boy yearly. See 2 Kings iii. 27, when King of Moab did it. See Balak's cry, Micah vi. 7. They thought like the poor heathen in India to-day. That is the worst of living amongst people who do not know or worship God. Take care of being much with godless people, else you will grow like them.

Would it be right for you to make such a vow? If you had made it, would it be right to keep it? No. It is a sin to break a vow; but it would be a worse sin to keep it after seeing that it was very wrong. But Jephthah did not see that it was very wrong. Only that it was very terrible and very painful to fulfil. He thought that God would approve of it. What do you think he should be blamed for? For his ignorance of God's character, in thinking that would please Him. He should have known better, and perhaps he could have known if he had not neglected God's teaching. But we do not know.

§ 3. Jephthah's Daughter

Now after the vow he goes to battle. Does he conquer? You know what happens after a great victory. Illuminations, rejoicing, crowds, and shouting and music, to welcome the conquerors. What delight and pride in the general's home, that all the nation were praising and thanking him. Only one young girl there, his only daughter—so glad, so proud—so fond of her father! She was watching for him, all unconscious of evil. The moment she saw him, out she rushed, dancing with joy, and sounding her song of triumph and of welcome. Oh, the pity of it! Can't you imagine the look of horror and agony in his eyes, as he started back from her? "Oh, alas, alas! my daughter. I have vowed to the Lord, and I cannot go back!" What a grand, heroic girl she was! Did she cry or scream, or beg to be let off? Not she! Poor ignorant girl, she, too, thought that God would require the vow to be kept. "Father," she said, "if you have vowed to the Lord, and the Lord has saved our people from the oppressor, keep your vow. I am willing to die for my country, and my father, and my God." Read Byron's poem:—

> "If my country, my God, oh, my sire,
> Demand that thy daughter expire."

And so she went out to die, this poor ignorant, loving, loyal Jewish girl. Was she right in thinking that God desired it? No. Human sacrifice was hateful to God. But, poor girl, she meant to do God's will, and only did in mistake that which was not God's will. Do you think God was pleased with her? I am sure He was. It was horrible, but it was grand. It was heroic self-sacrifice. And self-sacrifice with a righteous motive is very dear to the heart of God, however ignorant or mistaken it may be. It is the very essence of God's own nature, unselfishness—bearing and suffering for the sake of others. What was the grandest example of it in the whole world? Yes, when the blessed Saviour "for us men and for our salvation" came down from heaven and died on Calvary. Be thankful that you know more about God than this poor ignorant maiden; but be very sure that you can do no higher thing in His sight than to be utterly unselfish, to be willing to sacrifice everything for the sake of God and your brethren.

135

QUESTIONS FOR LESSON VI

Repeat the two-fold lesson and show it working out here.

Who were the new oppressors and the new deliverer?

Tell of Jephthah's awful vow.

Was it right?

Is there excuse for him?

Tell the touching story of Jephthah and his daughter meeting after the battle.

What do you think of Jephthah's daughter?

What do you mean by self-sacrifice?

What is the greatest instance of it in history?

LESSON VII

SAMSON—RESPONSIBILITY

Judges XIII. vv. 1-8, 24, 25, and XIV.

§ 1. *Samson's Dedication*

Repeat main lesson of Book of Judges.

Here is another story of another place and time. This chapter begins by telling of? What as usual followed the sin? Punishment. What nations already used for punishing? What nation now? *Describe Philistines, big, heavy, slow-witted, the butt of Israelites, etc. Try to make them stand out distinct and interesting.* Things again in bad state. Again God pities. How shown? A godly mother receives warning that son shall be born to play a great part in his people's history. What? (*v.* 5). Tell me of any other promise like this. (Abraham and Sarah, Hannah, Elisabeth, Virgin Mary.) He must be trained for this great future. How? What is a Nazarite? (Numbers vi. 2. One separated or dedicated unto the Lord). What were his vows? Distinguish from Nazarene. Is it not a lovely thought of the boy's life (*v.* 24). The child grew,

137

and the Lord blessed him. Poor Samson; what a pity that he should waste the blessing of God!

Is it not a solemn thing to be dedicated like Samson to a great work? Has anything like it been done to you? (Impress very solemnly the importance of Baptism.) That is your dedication. What are your vows? Has God any great work for you as for Samson? Any enemies to fight? Temper, lying, disobedience, etc. Anyone to be helped or delivered by you? Weak comrades tempted to carelessness, lying, drunkenness, etc. You to be God's Samson. Careless people sometimes excuse themselves, saying, "Not done any harm in the world." Is that a fair excuse? Why? Because we are vowed *to do good* —to be Christ's soldiers—to fight His battles—to make the world better and happier. He who is not doing that is an idler, a deserter.

§2. Samson's Home

Do you think those parents religious people? Were they anxious to rear up the boy aright? (*v.* 8). Their great aim for the boy, not that he should be rich and comfortable, and have an easy situation, but that he should be good and brave, and able to do God's work, to fight and, if necessary, die for his country and his God. What do you think should be the chief aim of parents for children? What should be the chief aim of boys and girls? What would you like to be? What business or profession? And you? And you? (*Don't be too solemn over this. Don't mind making them laugh. Tell perhaps of own childish aims and ideals. A little lightness may make following thought more impressive.)* In this future of yours should you like to be rich, happy? Is it wrong to wish this?

But what is the highest aim of all about one's future life? To do God's work in the world. To fight God's enemies. To deliver God's tempted children. To make this poor world brighter, and happier, and better for your being in it. *(In suitable classes the teacher might here speak of the great work of missions. So dear to Christ's heart—so undermanned. Parents straining and striving for every petty post of comfort and gain for their children and fretting—What to do with our boys? What to do with our girls? And the noblest work on earth waiting for helpers. Ask the class to pray that this Lesson, taught to-day in so many classes, may result in many resolves to offer themselves for this work.)* All work may and ought to be holy work. Therefore, pray about your future: "Lord, not so much that I may be rich, or great, or prosperous, but, above all, that I may be good. May do my duty in that state of life unto which it shall please God to call me."

§ 3. Disappointing God

Now picture that home, the awe-struck mother brooding over the mysterious future of her boy. Like what other? (Luke ii. 51). How she would pray for him! How proud she would be of his magnificent strength, and his daring deeds in camp of Dan (*v.* 25). What glorious hopes she would cherish for his future. Ah, you don't know how mothers' hearts are bound up in their children's future! What lovely, hopeful day-dreams they have for them! What a shame to disappoint them!

Here is this boy growing up—big boy now, moody, willful, keeping his outward Nazarite vow, yielding to his impulses in all else—self-will, disobedience. What was first great disappointment to parents? (xiv. 3). Now a man—going to marry. Not care if pleased God or parents. See his reply (*v.* 3). What a sad disappointment. The man who was to deliver Israel from brutal Philistines now going to marry into them. There will be no religion now; no godly family life like his father's. His wife would worship Dagon, and rejoice in Dagon's conquests over people of Jehovah. Her sympathies would be all with her own people, the conquerors. She would scorn the poor subject race. What a shame to disappoint his parents so bitterly! What a shame to disappoint God!

Is it possible to disappoint God? Ah, yes, God had designed great things for Samson's future if Samson had not spoiled it. God's plan about the Philistines was not overthrown. Even Samson's marriage over-ruled to further it. How? Wedding feast? Riddle—repeat it, and explain. A great wager on the riddle. Did they guess it? How? Was Samson angry? What did he do? So the Philistines more his enemies than ever. God's purpose not overthrown.

But how sorely Samson suffered all his life for that marriage. Look at the result in one week—a betrayed husband, a deserted wife, discord, strife, bloodshed; afterwards, a lonely, misguided, sinful life, captivity, blindness, violent death. No good, religious wife beside him to help and encourage him to better things. Don't you think when God sent him into the world and blessed him (xiii. 24) He designed something nobler and better for him than this poor wrecked life. Whose fault was it that he failed? God has good designs for you and me, too. Let us not disappoint Him.

There are other stories of him that we have not time for now. Tell me some briefly—how he killed the lion—set fire to the corn—how he carried off the gates of Gaza on his back; but they seem chiefly done to show off his strength or gratify his resentment. The great gift of strength was not used much for God, or for doing much good to Israel. He was very brave, and merry, and good-natured; but he seems to have quite wasted his opportunities and his gifts.

§ 4. Lessons

(1) *To be attractive and a favourite is not always a mark of goodness or of being pleasing to God.* Look at Samson—daring, merry-hearted, generous, attractive—a fine, big, good-natured fellow; full of fun; full of courage; dashing into the enemy without stopping to count them; playing mischievous tricks on the thick-headed Philistines; one of these men so attractive to others, who so easily becomes a leader of others. And yet no real character; no deep sense of duty or religion; no earnest struggle to put the Right before the Pleasant.

Is it a good thing for a boy to be a strong, brave, pleasant, good-natured fellow? (or, in a girls' class—a girl to be bright, merry, handsome, good-natured?) Yes. Makes him a favourite—a leader amongst others. These things are God's good gift to some boys. But he may have all these gifts, and not be a high character. What makes the high character that is pleasing to God? The effort to do the right even when it is unpleasant—putting God, and Right, and Duty first of all. Sometimes a poor, weak, puny, insignificant boy is a higher character than the other. Why? What makes his character higher? He is trying to fight down his temper or his cowardice, and to do what God wants, however hard it be. Yes, what God cares for most of all things in the world is the true, loyal struggle after the Right.

(2) *Responsibility for God's good gifts.* What gifts had God given to Samson? Size and strength, and influence amongst his companions. Why were they given? To make him fit to do the great work for which he was dedicated. Did he use them for this? No, we shall see in next lesson the sad result. Had he a right to use them as he liked himself? Why? Because they are God's, and given for a special purpose. If a man gave you money to use for him, would you have a right to use it as you liked for yourself? Is our case at all like Samson? Gifts of health, and brains, and perhaps pleasant, attractive disposition, and influence amongst our companions. They make us happier, and God likes that. But may we use them as we like? To do wrong things? To lead weaker ones astray? He who does that will be acting dishonourably, and grieving and disappointing God.

QUESTIONS FOR LESSON VII

Repeat the two-fold lesson.

Who were the new oppressors?

Tell of the dedication to God of the boy Samson.

What is like that in your life?

To whom are you dedicated?

Tell of Samson's marriage and his riddle.

Tell of the attractive things in Samson that made people admire him.

Who gave him these attractive gifts?

What was his fault that spoiled them all?

What is the lesson for us?

LESSON VIII

SAMSON—FAILURE

Judges XVI. v. 4 to end

This should be a most interesting and exciting subject if well handled. Read Milton's *Samson Agonistes*. Few writers have entered so thoroughly into the spirit of this story, and his vivid picturing will add much to the interest.

Pass over the first four verses of the chapter, merely mentioning the incident of the gates. Begin story at *v.* 4. There need be no hesitation about teaching very briefly the story of Delilah's treachery. She is described as a Philistine woman whom Samson loved in the same way perhaps as her whom he had married many years before. Don't tire the class with the application at the close. Try to carry the thought of it all through the Lesson. But if you have really roused and excited them, as you should have done, over the story, there will be need of making the application very short and direct, lest you lose their interest and spoil the lesson.

Recapitulate main lesson of last Sunday, *i.e.*,

Responsibility for God's gifts—remind of Samson's waste of them. When a man wastes God's gifts, he will lose them some day. See Parable of the Talents. See in Samson's case. We have seen several incidents of his life—the lion—the blazing corn—the gates of Gaza. We passed over a very generous act of self-sacrifice. (Tell briefly xv. 9-15.)

§ 1. The Traitress

To-day we are drawing toward the close of his brave, careless, wasted life. It is a dark, miserable story. As before his marriage, he is again deceived by a Philistine woman whom he loved. Poor foolish Samson trusted her. But she was a traitor, paid by the Philistines to entrap him (*v.* 5). Why not come and attack him openly? Ah! no—they had had enough of that already. Terribly afraid of him. So they bribed her to find out the secret of his strength, and had men hiding in another room to seize him at the fit time.

Did he tell her at once? No, told her untruths. What? Bind me with green withes—with new ropes—weave my long hair into the cloth with the shuttle. And at each time when he was tied she cried out what? What happened? Surely he should have known her treachery now. He should have gone away at once. But his will was very weak, though body was strong. He stayed on till at last, in a weak, foolish moment, she coaxed his secret from him. What was it? Yes. Then she waited till he was asleep, and then a man, who was hidden, stole softly out and shaved his head. Soon he awoke. What then? (*v.* 20). What an awful, horrible humiliation! What pain and misery and remorse! What delight to the Philistines to have him in their power! What did they do? They put out his eyes, and carried him off to dungeon in Gaza. Were they still afraid of his strength? Fetters of brass (*v.* 21).

What do you think was Samson's sin through which "the Lord departed from him"? Why should it matter that he let his head be shaved? I think it was because that was the sign of his Nazarite vow—the sign that he was dedicated to the Lord. The shaving of his head would indicate that his vow of dedication was over. He knew well the danger of this, but he could not bring himself to break away from the danger. He knew that his strength came through his Nazarite dedication to God, and that he had no right to risk it by such company as he was keeping. What is our dedication vow? (See *Baptismal vow*.) Take care lest we drop it as Samson did, not of deliberate intent, but by tampering with sin and keeping evil company. Like Samson we should lose all the God-given strength to be Christ's faithful soldiers and servants to our lives' end.

§ 2. *The Prison*

A great holiday in Gaza—shouting, rejoicing, chants of praise, bursts of barbaric music in the streets. A poor captive, blind and chained and miserable, listening in his dungeon. Oh, the agony and disgrace of it all as he thinks about the past—as he listens to the triumph song: "Praise unto Dagon, our god, who hath delivered our enemy into our hands." (*v.* 23). Imagine the wretched thoughts in his mind—of the old home—of the prayerful parents—of the Nazarite vow and the great gift of God, and the great plans God had for him. Israel's deliverer!

And now the promised deliverer lies blind and chained and grinding all day long at the wretched work of slaves. And God's great work is undone—and Israel is still oppressed. Poor wretched Samson! Don't you think they were bitter thoughts? And the bitterest thought of all would be, what? Try and think. Yes. "It is all my own fault! Oh, what a mad, wicked fool I have been!" Is it a good thing to think that it was his own fault—that he had been a wicked fool? Yes; when a poor sinner has found out that about himself, he is very near to finding out something very good about God. Perhaps poor Samson, in his lonely sorrow and pain, turned to God in real repentance. If so, would God cast him out? Did he ever cast a penitent out?

Did you ever know or hear of people in Samson's state? Sometimes poor old drunkard—or old sinner in the workhouse, once a healthy and prosperous man, but sinned away God's gifts, like Samson. Perhaps, in his misery, cried to God for forgiveness.

See Samson still grinding hard with his hands, and thinking and fretting hard in his soul. Suddenly the door opens—the shouts outside grow louder—a Philistine gaoler enters. "Samson, the lords and chiefs and people have sent for you: they want to see your strength; you are to come out and make sport for them." Fancy his fierce indignation. Those stupid Philistines, that used to fly before him in terror, now want to mock him, and make sport of him for their amusement. And he must go. He is blind and chained and weak. They could drag him with chains if he refused. Oh, the depth of shame and misery!

§ 3. The Catastrophe

Try to picture the scene. Great Temple of Dagon on the hillside, thousands of people shouting in triumph as the poor blind giant comes stumbling along with the brass chains on his mighty limbs. What fools those Philistines were to bring him out! They were probably too drunk to think about it. Hearts were merry (*v.* 25). And they did not know or think of what had happened in the prison. What? His strength was not in hair or muscles, but in his relation to God: his Nazarite vow broken when hair shaved. Perhaps, in sorrow for his sin and folly, he had now remembered his Nazarite vow to the Lord, and thus his strength returned. Now see great semicircle of seats like an enormous circus, and over it a roof resting on two front pillars, and on the top of it an enormous crowd too. How many? (*v.* 27). All cheering and laughing as Samson was tormented to make sport for them. You have seen a "strong man" performing, lifting weights in his teeth, bending iron bars, etc. Think of Samson like that before Philistines. It was a great triumph for Dagon, their god. They thought that they had now conquered God as well as Samson. And poor Samson had to feel that he had brought shame on God as well as on himself. Don't you think he would be very miserable? Do you think God cared for or pitied him in his misery? What! even after all his wrong-doing?

Samson seems tired. He is thinking. Ah! he is doing more; he is praying—very humbly, very earnestly. "Oh! Lord God, remember me, I pray Thee, and strengthen me *only this once*. I was sent to deliver Israel from these cruel Philistines, and I have shamefully failed. Oh! God, strengthen me only this once more. I don't want to escape; I am willing to die; but give me back my strength this once." And he turns to the boy that led him. "Lead me to the front pillars to rest myself." Carelessly the crowd watched him. But in a moment their old terror of Samson was roused. See that powerful grasp of the two big pillars. Hear the wild cry, "Let me die with the Philistines!" and then, with a mighty wrench, he has bowed himself forward, and tugged, and rocked, and shaken the huge pillars till they burst from their sockets. One awful crash—mad yells of terror—and Samson and the thousands of his enemies are lying dead together beneath the ruins. "The dead which he slew at his death were more than they which he slew in his life."

Poor Samson! Are you sorry for him? Whose fault was all the poor spoiled life? God's? Delilah's? No. All his own. What a grand career his might have been with the powers God gave him! What a poor, aimless, wretched, disappointing thing it was. And yet we are sorry for him. Do you think God was sorry? Do you think He forgave him? Certainly, if he repented, and asked to be forgiven. And I think he did. He is mentioned in Hebrews xi. as one of the heroes of faith. I like to think of that. We are inclined to dwell much on his faults. God saw his faults much more clearly than we do. But God was looking for the good that was there in spite of the faults, and taking hold of it, and by means of it lifting him to Himself. Is it not like a little epitaph on his grave this reference of inspired writer in Hebrews xi.: *"By faith Samson"*? Oh! God is so good and loving. He intended such good things for Samson, and he disappointed Him. Yet God did not cast him out. When He has intended grand things for you, and you sinfully fail of them, He tries not to cast you out. You can never *then* get the *best* thing which He intended. But He offers the *second* best, and if you fail of that, He offers the *third* best, and so on, as long as there is any hope for one at all. Is it not a shame to disappoint Him when He cares so for our good? How can you escape failing and disappointing Him?

QUESTIONS FOR LESSON VIII

Tell some of Samson's great deeds.

Who was Delilah? Of what nation?

Tell of her treacherous attempts to entrap Samson.

Tell of poor blind Samson in the mill.

Why was he a failure?

Do you think he was sorry?

Picture the great scene of his death.

What does his life teach us?

LESSON IX

SAMUEL—LENT UNTO THE LORD

1 Samuel I., II. to v. 11

§ 1. *The Last of the Judges*

What book of Bible just finished by us? What Judge last Lesson? (Briefly recapitulate.) Are we done with the judges now? No. Don't know how long this after Samson's time. But still in "the days of the Judges." Reading to-day of birth of "the last of the Judges," and the greatest of them all. Name? Yes. He was last of Judges. After him came the Kings. But he was greater than any of the Kings. He was the "King-maker." Remember Earl of Warwick, the "King-maker" in English history? Samuel—like him—raised up Saul, and deposed him, and put David in his place. Both Saul and David reverenced and feared him. What made him so great and so much reverenced? Because noble, and unselfish, and good—utterly devoted to God's service, therefore greatly used by God.

Can you see any reason in this chapter why he was so good? The reason that, above all others, has made good men always? Ah! yes—his mother. The greatest blessing in the whole wide world is a mother like Hannah. Sweet, and gentle, and unselfish—willing to give up all that she loves best in the world for the sake of seeing her boy a true servant of God.

§ 2. At Shiloh

Our story begins at the tabernacle at Shiloh. (See map.) There, after all the wanderings of Israel, the Ark of God at last rested in Joshua's days (Joshua xviii. 1) and there it remained up to the time of our story. It contained what? Therefore Shiloh was the great holy place—the great centre for the Church of Israel. Picture to yourselves this holy place on one of the great festival days of the year, like our Easter or Christmas.

A vast pilgrimage from all over the land—crowds and crowds gathering in for the great yearly feast-day, to worship before the Lord in Shiloh. Watch them crowding through the gates, men and women, old and young. One family especially. How many? Who? There they go with their holiday clothes in the holiday crowd. But do they look very happy? All? What was Hannah fretting about? Lonely home. No boys and girls running to her to make her glad. Something else? (*v.* 7). Yes, Peninnah, a jealous, spiteful woman, mocking at her in her loneliness and sorrow. Evidently not a very happy home. Not God's will to have two wives in a home. But the nations around had them, and the Israelites in those days did not know any better. You remember we have seen already how gradually people learned about God's will, and how patiently God waited and bore with them. (See Joshua, Lesson VIII.)

But Hannah has learned where to go in her trouble. All through the time of the sacrificial banquet she had to listen to the cruel gibes and mockery of Peninnah. They were torture to her; but she seems to have borne them meekly and gently. No doubt, God was training her by such struggles to be a true, noble woman—a mother worthy of bringing up so great a son. That is the good of all trouble, and vexation, and irritation, when borne nobly for sake of God and right. But she can bear it no longer. Her husband tries to comfort her. How? (*v.* 8). But in vain. She rises from the table and hurries out. Where to? Somebody sitting on the high priest's seat by a pillar as she passes on. Who? Yes. He was the judge and the high priest together. He had to rule the nation and rule the Church; but he could not rule his own family. And the poor old man sat with heavy heart watching the people as they came in, and feeling what sin and discredit to religion were caused by those wicked sons of his, whom he had made clergy of the Church. He could hear them greedily demanding gifts; he could see that there was less reverence for God, and more drunkenness and sin of every kind in those yearly pilgrimages to Shiloh. And he knew the cause. Poor old father, like many another father, breaking his heart about his wicked sons.

Even as he watches he sees a woman hurry in with flushed face and flashing eyes. What does he think?

(*v.* 13). He sees her throw herself down, sobbing before the altar, and raising her eyes to heaven, and moving her lips. "Surely she is drunk," said the old man, and he turns to her angrily. "Get away with your drunkenness; put away thy wine from thee." What a cruel wrong to the heart-broken woman, who had cast herself down in the very passion of her sorrow and her longing for God's comfort: "O Lord, remember me, and pity me, and send me a little son, and I will give him up to Thy service all the days of his life." Must not blame the poor high priest too much for his mistake. The poor old man had a sore heart himself—therefore he spoke hastily and sharply—and he was sorry for his mistake in a moment. "Nay, my lord, I am not drunk," she said, "but have been pouring out my soul before the Lord." Did he keep on being angry? (*v.* 17). No; he blessed her, and prayed that God would grant her petition. And with comfort in her heart—the comfort that always comes from true communion with God—she went her way, and did eat, and was no more sad (*v.* 18).

§ 3. *The Child's Training*

A year has passed. It is again the day of the great pilgrimage to the Feast of Tabernacles, and Eli is again watching the people. There is Elkanah—perhaps he remembers him—but where is Hannah? Away in her mountain home at Arimathea, minding her baby boy! Oh, what a glad, thankful heart she has as she holds him in her arms and plays with him, and thinks, like all the mothers in the world, that there never, never was a brighter, cleverer, lovelier baby since the world began. Poor fond little mother. They are nearly all the same as that. Thank God for the big, loving hearts that He has given them.

But many a fond mother is a very foolish one, and has very low notions of what makes the highest good for her child. Many a mother thinks only of her boy getting on, and being rich, and by-and-by having a nice house and a good business, or a high name in the world. Are they good things? Yes; but you may have all these and be very miserable, and be a poor, contemptible creature, too. What is the real treasure of life to seek for one's child? What will make him noble, and good, and happy beyond all things else? You remember how our Lord puts it: "Seek ye first"—what? (Matthew vi. 33).

That is what Hannah did. All the time she was playing with her little boy she was thinking of her high hopes for him, and lifting up her heart to God for him. She was remembering the vow she had made that day in the tabernacle that her boy should be God's servant as long as he lived. Oh! it is good to think of that sweet, stainless boyhood lived so close to God, and of the earnest, loving mother, whose highest ambition for her child was that he should be a noble, God-like man, given up unto the Lord. What is the most powerful thing in God's world? I think the prayers and tears of a mother for a child. I don't think God *can* leave them unanswered, so deeply do they touch Him. In this world or in the world to come they must be somehow answered. It is a very blessed thing, but it is a very solemn thing, to have a holy, praying mother!

§ 4. Lent unto the Lord

Three years more have passed and Elkanah and Hannah are at Shiloh again with the crowds of people. But who is with them now? A tiny boy, about four years old, just beginning to speak distinctly. Poor little chap, he is to be left in Shiloh, to live in the tabernacle, and learn to attend on Eli. So very young to be without his mother? Was it not hard for him? But, oh! think what it was to his mother to leave him! How simply it reads in the story that she brought up her boy to Shiloh, and presented him to God, and that she made a little coat, and brought it up every year at her annual visit.

But just think what it meant—to bring up her little boy, and leave him—to go back to the little mountain home to cry about him, and think about him every day and night for a year—to make a little coat for him, and work into that little coat all her love, and pain, and anxiety, and hopes—to look forward for twelve long months to her coming up again to take him in her arms once more, to try to quiet for one brief day the hungry craving of her heart. But her heart was full of love and thankfulness to God, who had so loved and blessed her and her little son. Nothing less would satisfy her than the complete consecrating of her boy to God.

> "I give thee to thy God—the God that gave thee—
>   To be a spring of gladness to my heart!
>   And precious as thou art,
>   And pure as dew of Hermon, He shall have thee,
>   My own—my beautiful—my undefiled,
>   And thou shalt be His child!"

And so blessed was this self-sacrifice for God, that she actually sang a beautiful song of thanksgiving in the midst of her pain. Look at it (ch. ii., *vv.* 1-11), like the song of the Blessed Virgin, as we find it in the Magnificat. God always gives gladness to great self-sacrifice like that.

Your parents, too, have consecrated you to God. When? Baptism. "To be Christ's faithful soldier and servant unto his life's end." Some parents have forgotten it. Some, like Hannah, remember it always, and pray to God always to make use of their boy and girl. Sometimes, as with Hannah, it means a great wrench. I know of boys and girls called out to God's work to teach the heathen, and it was hard to let them go, perhaps to see them no more. But it has been done; it may be what God will want done for some of you—the blessedest life in the whole world for you. Sometimes it may be but to serve God faithfully at home. Pray to God earnestly that, whether at home or abroad, He will keep you consecrated to Himself—granted unto the Lord.

QUESTIONS FOR LESSON IX

Who was "the last of the Judges"?

Picture in words his mother's visit to the church.

Who was Eli?

How did he mistake her?

Tell of her next visit three years later. What for?

How can a mother to-day follow her example?

LESSON X

THE CALL OF SAMUEL

Samuel II. 26-30, and III.

§1. *The Child at Shiloh*

Remember last Lesson—last heard of Samuel? Little boy left by his mother to attend upon Eli, to minister in the temple. God had great purposes for that little boy. He was to be what? A Judge, a Prophet, a Leader, a King-maker. But it is not as any of these we usually think of him. Ever see picture of him? What like? Little boy kneeling in white robe beside his cot in prayer to God, or listening to God. "Speak, Lord, for Thy servant heareth." (*v.* 10). Hear of this to-day.

Bigger boy now; perhaps ten or twelve (Josephus, *Antiquities of the Jews* x. 4). Has been for years doing little deeds of service, lighting the sanctuary lamps, opening the doors, tending the priests, joining perhaps with little choir-boys, in his white surplice or ephod, singing the praises of God, doing little humble, childlike things in God's service; and then at night, when he had trimmed the lamps, going off to his little chamber

158

beside the church to sleep. Evidently priest's rooms off the tabernacle. His room near to Eli.

What is said about God's word, or message? (*v.* 1). It was precious, or *rare*—no prophet vision—perhaps because the men who should have received God's teaching for the people were too wicked to be trusted with it. People could not hear God's will. But God was preparing a prophet for them now.

§ 2. God's Call

Eli getting very old—shown in *v.* 2? Poor Eli! getting old, and with big sorrow in his heart. Why? Sons can give great pain to a father. These were very bad sons. Contrast with Samuel ii. 26, *vv.* 27-30. Partly father's fault—should not have let them be priests. And so God had had to warn him long before (*v.* 27). But no use—sons too wicked—old father too weak and cowardly. Think of him lying in bed, with his poor dim eyes wakeful in the darkness, and his poor sad heart thinking about his misery, wishing perhaps that his boys had been like that gentle, lovable boy who was sleeping in the little room so near. Suddenly hears curtain moving, child's footsteps, and in a moment the boy in his night-dress is beside him. "Here I am, sir; you called me." He had been wakened by a voice, and thought the poor old man wanted something. "No, my son, I did not call you; lie down again." Again silence; the wakeful old priest fretting over the pain and fear in his conscience; the innocent boy lying peacefully in his bed. What next? Yes—rushes in again. "Here I am, sir; you surely called me this time." Had he? No. Do you think Eli wondered? Do you think his conscience frightened him? He remembered the warning of God (ii. 27). What could be this strange call to the child that nobody else heard? And then in a few minutes the boy rushes in again, this time startled and excited. "No mistake this time; I certainly was called."—And then Eli perceived—what? Think of his wonder—prophets had ceased—no one for years had had revelation from God. What did he tell Samuel to do?

Think of the awfully solemn feeling of the boy. Would you have been frightened? Probably Samuel was, too, a little. But he was a true-hearted, innocent boy, with a clear conscience, and, therefore, probably not very much afraid. But think of him going back where the mysterious Voice was, and getting into bed. Do you think he would feel sleepy? Too excited, wondering. What a terrible message! What was it? Do you think he slept much after it? No; pain of telling his kind old friend, and the wonder and awe of thinking—"God has spoken to me. Am I to be a prophet, or what is the meaning of it all?" Picture the boy at daylight lying in his bed, pale, strained, excited, trying to delay meeting with Eli.

At last Eli heard him opening the doors, and he called him. See how he calls him, "My son." I think he was very fond of that boy. I wonder why he did not call him earlier. Must have been curious to know what God said. Why, do you think? Perhaps afraid; had not clear, innocent conscience like Samuel; perhaps remembered God's warning (ii. 27), and feared this might be announcing the punishment. (See Josephus, *Antiquities of the Jews* x. 4.) Was it? Are you sorry for poor old man? How sore to hear! How touchingly resigned he was (*v.* 18).

§ 3. *Lesson*

"Them that honour Me I will honour, and they that despise Me shall be lightly esteemed." See a boy honouring God, putting duty and religion foremost as the chief things in life. Same in his manhood. All through his beautiful life he honoured God, and never was there a judge in Israel more honoured than he. Religion always makes an honoured life.

See Eli's sons, despised God, grew up bad, godless boys, bad, godless men. Ever see such men respected and honoured? They that despise God are lightly esteemed.

QUESTIONS FOR LESSON X

What was old Eli's family sorrow?

Are there such sorrows to-day? Whose fault?

Tell of God's call to the child Samuel.

Did he like meeting Eli in the morning? Why?

Which would be happier—Hannah or the mother of Eli's boys?

What do you think is the chief happiness or sorrow of any mother?

LESSON XI

THE GLORY DEPARTED

1 Samuel IV.

§ 1. *The Battle of Ebenezer*

Remember the old prophet's warning from God to Eli? (ch. ii. 33, 34). Message by Samuel? (iii. 12-15). Poor Eli! what a troubled heart he must have had as he thought of God's displeasure and threatenings!

This chapter tells of a terrible battle—with whom? When heard of last? Evidently recovered their strength again, to oppress Israel, but Israel strong enough to fight. So the two armies met at Ebenezer. What had always been source of Israel's success? Had they God's favour now? Why? Very corrupt and wicked. Evil priests' example made them still worse. God's favour cannot go with willful sin. The important thing with God is not what we *say* or what we *do*, but what we ARE. Righteousness is the most important thing in our life. Nothing else can make up for it. God would not help these wicked Israelites. What was result of battle? (*v.* 2).

A similar case before? (Joshua vii. 4-6). What did Joshua do? (*v.* 6). God's reply? (*v.* 11). So again now this same cause. Did the elders inquire about their sins? What would be the right way to win back God's favour? Inquiry and penitent sorrow. What way did they try? (*vv.* 3-5). No permission from God to do such a thing; but they remember the presence of the Ark, when Jordan divided, and Jericho fell. Superstitiously they think God's presence *must* go with Ark. If take Ark into battle, God *is bound* to save it and them. They were, therefore, very anxious to get this outward sign of God's presence, while very careless as to the righteousness of character which would really win God's presence for them. So Hophni and Phinehas brought them the Ark, perhaps against old Eli's will. And when the beaten Israelites saw it come, they shouted with a great shout, and frightened the Philistines. What did these say? (*vv.* 7, 8). Had they reason to be frightened? No; God's favour and help had been driven away from Israel by sin. The Ark a mere empty, useless thing without that; an "outward sign" without the "inward grace." Result? (*v.* 11).

§ 2. *The Death of Eli*

Scene changes to Shiloh. Eli sitting in his chair of office at the gate, watching the road for tidings; his heart trembling for his sons, but still more for the safety of the Ark. All the people remaining in Shiloh anxious and excited. But Eli's trouble was the worst, conscience reproving him for these wicked sons whom he had reared; perhaps, too, for the Ark let out of his keeping. Messengers like Joshua's (Lesson X), like the messengers of Roderick Dhu in *Lady of the Lake.* Like those in 1 Samuel viii. 11; 2 Samuel xv. 1; xviii. 19, etc. Swift, panting runner dashes breathless through the gate, in deep mourning, clothes rent, and ashes on his head. Surely bad news. Hear the wild cries, and questionings, and lamentations; "all the city cried out."

Two people to whom this bad news was to be fatal? Imagine the poor trembling old man as he listens. How old? Could he see messenger? Think of him as the messenger is being brought to him; the swift thoughts rushing through his mind of the old prophet's message (ii. 32-35), and Samuel's vision (ch. iii.). He can't see the rent clothes or the ashes on head; but he knows by the "noise of the crying" (the word signifies any confused noise, like the splashing of rain, or the din made by a multitude of people) that it was bad news. "Tell me what is done, my son;" and he tells him four things, each worse than the previous one. What? Which of the four killed him? Why? The sign of God's presence was gone from the Church and the nation. It had gone because of Israel's sin, and he and his sons were largely to blame for it. Poor old man! though he was so greatly to blame, we must pity and respect him for his love to the Ark, the sign of God's presence. This loss was to him worse even than the death of his sons.

Another heart, too, was broken by the news. A pious young mother with her new-born babe. Who? Wicked husband had brought sorrow upon her by his evil life. Worse sorrow, now that she was a lonely widow. But, like her old father-in-law, she also felt that the worst sorrow was God's displeasure. The glory departed. The sign of the Divine Presence gone for ever. What did she call her child? Meaning? What a very dark, sad ending to the glory of Eli and his family.

§ 3. Lessons

I.—*Against Superstition*. It was God's presence and favour—not the Ark, the mere symbol of it—that was of importance. So with Church and Sacraments. The Church is as God's Ark in the world. But if it ever became so utterly corrupt that God had to leave it, there would be no help in it. The Sacraments are God's means of bestowing grace and strength on us; but it is possible by our sin to destroy their effect. It is possible to have been baptized, and afterwards to lose all the grace of Baptism. And it is possible for a careless, godless person to receive of the Holy Communion, and be none the better of it, but rather worse. Like the Israelites with the Ark in the battle of Aphek, it is possible to think superstitiously of the Church and the Sacraments as if they were mere charms, by which we can force God to be present with us.

II.—*The worst trouble on earth is to be abandoned by God.* Whether with nation or Church, or with individual man. No other trouble as terrible as that. What would be the greatest affliction that could come on any Church? Poverty? Loss of position? No. If it were only money and position was lost—if they did not lose or forsake God—if the Ark, the presence of

165

God remained—the rest would not matter so very much. A Church faithful to God would weather the storm, weakened and impoverished, indeed, in outward appearance, but probably purer, more loyal, more faithful to God, through the trouble that had come upon her, and rejoicing more in the devotion of her children than at any time before. Suppose all her riches and position had remained, and her clergy and people had grown corrupt like Israel, *there* would be the real trouble—the Ichabod—the glory departed. So also in the individual life. Boy, girl, man, woman, the only hopeless calamity is the driving away God by our sinful, disobedient lives. If God's favour be with us, if we are still trusting and following Him, it is possible to bear calmly even great earthly troubles. But all the wealth of the world would not compensate for the loss to an evil, selfish, Christless life, that has driven out God. Its glory has departed. Take care of your lives. You have been consecrated to God as children. Learn that the worst of all dangers is the danger of slipping away from Him. Pray Psalms li. 11: "Take not Thy Holy Spirit from me."

QUESTIONS FOR LESSON XI

Who were now Israel's oppressors?

When before?

Tell of the battle of Ebenezer.

What was the Ark of God?

Why did they carry it into battle?

Did it save them? What happened?

Will Church or Sacraments help us if our hearts are wrong?

Illustrate, *e.g.,* in Holy Communion.

Tell the touching story of Eli's death.

LESSON XII

THE HAND OF GOD

1 Samuel V. and VI.

Last lesson about terrible defeat, capture of the Ark, the slaughter of 30,000 men. Even worse things we learn from other parts of Scripture—Shiloh sacked and burned, and its people massacred by the victorious Philistines (see Psalm lxxviii. 60-64; Jeremiah vii. 12, and xxvi. 9). Probably some of the "lost books" kept at Shiloh, then destroyed—Book of Jasher (Joshua x. 13), Book of the Wars of the Lord (Numbers xxi. 14). A terrible trouble, indeed, had Israel brought on itself by its sin.

§ 1. Dagon

Now the scene changes. We turn away from burnt town and weeping people and desolate sanctuary. We see in the land of the Philistines a great festivity—a grand religious procession. Great is the rejoicing at the gates of Ashdod, great the shouts and praises of Dagon, their god. Dagon has conquered Jehovah. He has taken

168

Him captive. Into his temple shall the mysterious Ark be brought.

Do you remember a former religious rejoicing before Dagon? (Lesson VIII). Dagon and the Philistines did not come off best that time—should have remembered it. But no; they were so proud of carrying off "the Israelite God," they would put the Ark at the feet of Dagon, to celebrate Dagon's power. Poor ignorant idolators: how little they knew when they could think thus of the Almighty God, the Father of all men.

Ever see picture of mermaid? Dagon like that—human body, ending in a fish. Imagine people actually worshipping and praying to an ugly, silly-looking image such as that, like the poor ignorant heathen in India and Africa to-day. You have seen pictures of the ugly brass and wooden idols which they worship, not in love, but in fear. They pray to them and do them honour chiefly because they believe them to be evil, and to have evil power, and to be able to do great mischief if vexed. What a miserable, horrible religion: all dread, all darkness. None of the comfort, and love, and happiness that come from the knowledge of God and of the story of our Blessed Lord. Does God feel more of anger or of pity for them? Remember our Lord's pity for them, and His command to all Christians (Matthew xxviii. 19). God taught these idolators a lesson about their idols? (*v.* 3). And again? (*v.* 4). Yes; head and hands off, nothing but the fish-stump left, lying, a dead, ugly lump of wood or brass, on the floor. How could they think that poor, degraded thing to be a god? (See *v.* 5). Curious trace of this story in Zephaniah i. 9—"those that leap on," or, more correctly, "leap over the threshold." How terrified the priests and people of Ashdod! They had heard of this Ark at the crossing of Jordan and the fall of Jericho and the smiting of Egypt (ch. iv. 8; vi. 6). Now Dagon lay smashed—perhaps they could bear that—but horrible sores came on them, and perhaps swarms of field-mice in their corn (ch. vi. 5). Must get rid of this awful Ark. But not like to lose such a proof of their victory: perhaps it would be quiet at Gath or at Ekron. What happened? Surely they should have learned God's power now, and turned to pray to Him. But they thought perhaps that He was only the Jews' God, and would not receive Philistines. Were they right?

§ 2. *The Tragedy of Bethshemesh*

Scene changes again. A harvest day at Bethshemesh—thousands of reapers working amid the golden cornfields. Suddenly a shout of surprise, of rejoicing—a wild, glad rush from the harvest-field out on the southern road. What did they see? Tell me the story of the cart and the two cows who had come without guide or driver all the way to Bethshemesh. Was it a strange thing for cows to do? Not really so, for all animals are constantly doing God's will—their powers, instincts, passions, desires, all given by God—their acts are the doing of what God wants done on earth. It was very easy, therefore, to make these two cows do God's special will here. And the five Philistine lords who had followed the cart—why? (*v.* 9)—they now learned that all was of God, and not of chance.

See the rejoicing at Bethshemesh, the great stone (*v.* 14) turned into an altar, cart broken up, the sacrifice offered of praise to Jehovah; and after the sacrifice of course, there would be a feast. And then an awful thing happened. Heated perhaps with wine and feasting, they lost all sense of reverence, and encouraged each other to look into the Ark and examine its contents. The priests and Levites of the town (*v.* 9) knew the duty of reverence, and the danger of contempt for religion; but the whole nation seems to have been degraded, and unfit for God's Ark or God's presence amongst them. What a number of them must have sinned! It seems that seventy men were struck dead for the irreverence. Of course, the number in the text must be a mistake. Explain that numbers were denoted, as with us, by letters of alphabet, and that dots over letters greatly increased the number meant, so that mistakes in numbers could very easily take place. The Hebrew reads, "seventy men, fifty thousand men," which does not make sense, and must be a mistake. In a country village such as Bethshemesh, the whole population would not be very many, and probably those who looked into the Ark were a very small portion of them. Josephus in his History, says "seventy men;" and some Hebrew manuscripts have same number.

§ 3. Lessons

I.—The danger of irreverent conduct towards the All Holy, Almighty God.

II.—The misery and degradation of Idolatry. Think of the poor ignorant Philistines, and the mutilated fish-stump of Dagon. Think of the horrible worship in India and Africa, and the sad, hopeless lives, with no knowledge of God—of heaven—of resurrection. Think of a funeral—heart-broken mother and her dead child and nothing to give comfort or hope. Think of the desire of our Lord (Matthew xxviii. 19), and the blessedness of going out to do His will, and comfort and gladden those wretched lives. Perhaps the high privilege from God will come to some of you that you may go. Would you like to go? Would the Lord like you to go?

QUESTIONS FOR LESSON XII

Tell of Philistines rejoicing in their idol temple. What for?

Name of the idol?

They thought it had conquered Israel's God. Why?

Where are idols still worshipped? Tell anything you know about them.

Which would God be—angry or sorry about it?

What does He wish His church to do?

How can you be of any help?

LESSON XIII

THE REFORMATION

1 Samuel VII.

The last three Lessons told of sad decline in religion—God forgotten—idols worshipped—people irreligious—even the priests of Shiloh so utterly vile that they but contaminated the people. So God's favour lost, and punishment incurred. Remember defeat at Aphek—destruction of Shiloh—capture of Ark—glory departed, Israel degraded, hopeless, crushed—oppressed—courage, and righteousness, and hope vanished together. Repeat "Two-fold Lesson" of Book of Judges. We have come again to the same old circle—Sinning: Punishment; but now the other two things—Repenting: Deliverance—are soon to follow.

§ 1. *Repentance*

Wretched state of Israel. All religious services probably ceased after destruction of Shiloh and capture of Ark. Like the days of Papal interdict in England in time of King John. Saddened and troubled, the people began to long again for God's favour. Conscience began to stir; there arose a wistful, sorrowful desire for the God of their fathers; they felt "the time long" (*v.* 2); remembered God's goodness in former repentances—the return of Ark (*v.* 1) fanned the flickering flame of hope. Perhaps God would forgive them!

Then, like John Baptist, Samuel appears, preaching repentance, bidding them destroy the idols, promising them God's favour and deliverance from their oppressors (*v.* 3). Like Moses and Joshua. All true prophets must teach that God will not take our part while disloyal to Him.

Long since we have heard of Samuel—when last? Evidently he had escaped when Shiloh destroyed. Now many years passed; he is a grown man, but still a faithful servant of God. Not every religious child grows to be a religious man. It was still Samuel's cry, "Speak, Lord, for Thy servant heareth." See what a power for good he was. Men who put God and righteousness first are always of powerful influence for good. People must respect and attend to them.

Like the Huguenot pastors in France, he had probably to move secretly, through fear of Philistines, hiding in the caverns—showing himself now in one place, now in another; gradually rousing Israel to see the greatness of their sins and the goodness of God. And so repentance, and fresh, new spiritual life, began amongst them, and with it the patriotic resolve to be free from Philistine yoke.

174

How did they show reality of repentance? (*v.* 4). Talking about religion, and saying, "We have sinned," is not enough. It is by acts that real earnestness is shown. Was God willing to forgive? Glad to forgive?

§ 2. *The National Assembly*

Now, at last, Samuel thinks they may venture on a National Assembly to meet openly and declare for God, and discard Philistine idols. It was a great risk. It would certainly bring down the Philistines on them. Defeat would be terrible in their defenseless state. And Samuel was no warrior, like Gideon or Jephthah. He was but a righteous man—a holy prophet. All he could do was, "I will pray to Jehovah." (*v.* 5). This meeting at Mizpeh would terribly test their faith.

The day of assembly has come. From town and village, from mountain and valley, see the poor scattered people gathering timidly to Mizpeh. They knew the danger, but their trust in God was returning. And Samuel promised what? (*v.* 5). What was there besides prayer? Fasting and public confession to God: "We have sinned against the Lord." And then the pouring out of water—perhaps an expression of humiliation—perhaps a form of swearing loyalty to God henceforth. A touching sight, yet a stirring, inspiriting sight—these bands of Israel sorrowing for their sin, and pledging themselves for the future to a righteous life—"to do justly, and love mercy, and walk humbly with their God." Surely a glad sight for God. Surely there was joy in the presence of angels of God, etc. (Luke xv. 10).

Ah! soon came the testing time of their faith. What? (*v.* 7). Did they trust themselves? Did they trust God? (*v.* 8). Tell me their request. Was it heard? Yes, and new power and courage came to these poor frightened men. They saw the powerful army coming to destroy them. But they heard the thunder of heaven rolling overhead. Like many children amongst ourselves, thunder seemed to them the voice of God (ch. ii. 10). Jehovah thundered with a great voice (so Hebrew) and roused to joyful enthusiasm by that voice, they dashed down headlong upon the coming foe. What matter the poor armour, the smallness of numbers? What matters anything now, if God is on their side again? The force of the wild rush breaks the lines of the Philistines. A panic seizes them. They turn and flee for their lives to the shelter of Bethcar. What glad hearts they were that raised the Ebenezer (*v.* 12). What thankfulness to the kind and merciful God. What happiness that they had now returned to His service.

§ 3. Lessons

I.—*The courage, and peace, and hopefulness, that come of repentance and forgiveness.* Illustrate, child forgiven by mother, and received back to favour. In turning to the Lord, and seeking His forgiveness, every man in Israel was conscious of right-doing, and conscious of God's restored friendship. The moral support of such consciousness is great to everyone. We saw in previous Lessons how misery, and weakness, and cowardice came of forsaking God. We see here how courage and happiness came of return to Him. That is what gave the courage to charge upon the enemy. Remember, no real peace or courage away from God. All peace and courage by keeping close to Him.

II.—*The way to victory.* What was the result of this turning to God? Not only victory at Mizpeh? (*vv.* 13, 14). So with us. If have sinned and lost heart, and find it hard to be good, turn like Israelites in penitence and prayer. Evil will attack again, and fight hard for the mastery. Like the Philistines, who did not want to let Israel go. But let there be prayer, and faith, and honest desire for consecration to God, and victory is sure. It must be so, since He is more desirous of our victory than are we ourselves. "They that trust in the Lord are as Mount Zion, which cannot be moved."

QUESTIONS FOR LESSON XIII

What was the state of Israel in Samuel's early days?

Did he try to deliver them by fighting like the other judges?

What did he think most important?

How did he begin his reformation?

Tell of great national religious gathering. What did they promise?

What happened in next battle?

Do you think their repentance had anything to do with this?

What is the secret of real confidence and courage in troubles?

LESSON XIV

SELF-WILL AND GOD'S WILL

1 Samuel VIII.

§ 1. *Wanting To Be Like Others*

Samuel at Ramah, at the old home of his infancy, where erected altar unto the Lord (ch. vii. 16, 17). In that home Elkanah and Hannah had lived and worshipped God. In that place Joseph of Arimathea lived in the years long afterwards. Probably after ruin of Shiloh (previous Lesson) Samuel had retired there, and probably for years remained, like Paul at Damascus, in quiet, lonely preparation by God for his great life work. During this time of his retreat probably took place Samson's wild actions and fitful victories and tragic death. Then Samuel began to move secretly amongst the down-trodden people, and to rouse their spirit to religion and to patriotism (previous Lesson). And now, as judge and chief of the nation, he still lived in the old home, taking his journeys "on circuit," like our own judges to-day, to judge Israel.

One day a deputation of chiefs to Ramah to see

178

the old leader, now probably sixty or seventy years old. What did they want? (*v.* 5). What two reasons had they? Ever before wanted king, and what answer did they get? (Judges viii. 22, 23). Gideon's answer must be remembered—God was their King. That was the magnificent thought that always raised them high above level of all other nations, and gave such grandeur and nobleness to their history. Righteousness and holiness, not mere earthly pomp, was to be their ideal. Now they were anxious not so much for God and holy leaders who should be God's servants, God's Lieutenants, but a king who should be a soldier to fight for them, and to rule them in pomp, like whom? (*v.* 5, *v.* 20)—"like all the nations," *i.e.*, the heathen, Canaanites, Philistines, etc. Their glory used to be that they were *unlike* these nations.

Show here that many sins come amongst young people from wanting to be "like other people." Boys want to be like comrades, who are often very bad examples—girls who would like to be religious, are ashamed because not "like others." Remember, you are members of the Kingdom of God—"the Lord your God is your King." Dare to be singular, to stand alone; never mind what anyone says.

Had these people any right on their side? Yes. Samuel old. His sons not good men. Philistines still a danger. Besides, God had almost promised king (Deuteronomy xvii. 15-20). What then was wrong? They had determined to have a king when they themselves thought fit, *without consulting God's will.* They did not value their religious privileges; thought more of pomp and fighting than of

179

religion and God. They were dissatisfied with God's arrangement for them—impatient and presumptuous and self-willed. We know from *vv.* 7, 8, that in his own good time God would probably have given king, but not just yet. What should they have done? Come in prayer to God, seeking His will, and saying, "Thy will be done"; "We should like a king, but God knows best."

§ 2. Samuel's Religion

You see that was what Samuel did. Was he pleased at their demand? (*v.* 6); vexed, irritated. It was a slight on him who had been so true and faithful; but worse, it was a slight on God. He could not understand anyone questioning God's decisions. But, angry as he was, did he refuse them at once or turn them away? What? (*v.* 6.) Prayed; leaves all decision to God. See the effect on him. Vexed and irritated, he went to God. He came forth a different man after communion with God; calm, quiet, restful. God had given him relief and sympathy, for He shared in his disappointment—submission to the Divine will—strength to bear the insult to himself. Wonderful what prayer can do. "Habitual prayer constantly confers decision on the wavering, energy on the listless, calmness on the excitable, disinterestedness on the selfish." Learn to live much in prayer and communion with God, to come to Him with every trouble and vexation. "Thou wilt keep him in perfect peace whose mind is stayed on Thee."

See here the sweet, innocent religion of the child had developed into the noble, unselfish religion of the man. Now that he knew God's will about it, he was satisfied. No thought for himself or for his sons. He was possessed of almost kingly power; his sons were in high and prosperous positions. But a man who lives much in God's presence thinks not of such considerations in the face of duty. In his high-souled patriotism and generosity, and his desire to do the will of God, he at once put himself and his sons aside. What matter about self, if only good comes to others, if only the will of God be done on earth as it is done in heaven? Remember a great New Testament example of this disinterestedness? John Baptist. "He must increase, I must decrease: this my joy therefore is fulfilled."

Sadly he warned them of what they are bringing on themselves. Firmly he showed them of God's disapproval. But then he left them to choose. Did they ask that God should decide for them? (See *vv.* 19, 20.) "No," they said, "we *will* have a king. We want to have our own way." When grown men capable of deciding say such things, God often lets them have their way. It is often the only way to teach them their mistake. See parable of prodigal demanding, "Give me the portion of goods," etc. Poor fellow, how bitterly he learned in the far country that it would have been better to stay with his father. So nowadays, too. It is a terribly dangerous thing to set up your will against God. "I must have my own way about choice of life-work, or about this or that smaller decision." Oh, you may force God to teach you your mistake by a very bitter lesson. Pray, "Thy will, not mine, O Lord!"

Here we have to say good-bye to Samuel. In next

course of lessons he comes in again, and we shall see how nobly he acted towards the new king, who had displaced him. Free from every trace of jealousy, he exalted Saul to the uttermost, and loved him, and took him to his heart as a son. He pleaded with him, and advised him, and strove to save him from his evil dispositions. And when at last, with a sore heart, he had to pronounce the sentence of God's rejection on him, he went home to his lonely house at Ramah to mourn for that young king who had so spoiled his life. The story of the kings and the kingdom begins in next course of lessons, for Samuel the prophet was

"THE LAST OF THE JUDGES."

QUESTIONS FOR LESSON XIV

Now Samuel is an old man ruling Israel. What did the people demand of him?

Who did Samuel say was their real King?

Did Samuel like their demand?

How would it affect him personally?

Was that what he most cared about?

To whom did he go for guidance?

What lesson here for us?

Now we are done with the Judges. Next lessons begin the story of the Kings.

CPSIA information can be obtained
at www.ICGtesting.com
Printed in the USA
BVHW071920100822
644253BV00003B/403